# COLLEGE.EDU

. . . . . . . . . . . . . . . . . . . . . .

## Online Resources for the Cyber-Savvy Student

VERSION 11.0
LISA@LISAGUERNSEY.COM
(LISA GUERNSEY)

OCTAMERON
ASSOCIATES

**Address correspondence to:**

Octameron Associates
PO Box 2748
Alexandria, VA 22301
703. 836. 5480 (voice)
703. 836. 5650 (fax)

www.octameron.com
octameron@aol.com

ISBN 1-57509-121-6
PRINTED IN THE UNITED STATES OF AMERICA

Many thanks to my husband, Rob,
for his wired advice and unwavering support.

# TABLE OF CONTENTS

## Part One: Getting Plugged In

**Chapter 1:** Site Seeing: The Basics ........................................................ 8

**Chapter 2**: Connecting and Communicating ..................................... 10
  Connecting .......................................................................... 10
  Communicating ........................................................................ 11

## Part Two: Search, Snoop, and Select

**Chapter 3:** Searching Online Databases .......................................... 16
  Collecting Information About Colleges ......................................... 16
  Looking for Specific Types of Schools ........................................... 21
  Finding and Using College Home Pages ...................................... 22

**Chapter 4:** Snooping for the Real Story ........................................... 26
  Getting the Latest College News .................................................. 26
  Getting the Regional Scoop ......................................................... 28
  Thinking About Safety ................................................................. 29
  What About College Rankings? .................................................... 29
  Thinking Critically ....................................................................... 30

**Chapter 5:** Selecting the Best Schools for You .................................. 32
  Preparing for a Campus Tour—The Real Thing ............................ 32
  Taking a Campus Tour—Virtually ................................................. 33
  Gathering More Advice ................................................................ 35
  Using Forums .............................................................................. 37
  Do Some Interviews of Your Own ................................................ 38

**Chapter 6:** Considering Distance Education and Co-op .................... 40
  Learning About Distance Education ............................................. 40
  A Sampling of Distance Education Programs ............................... 43
  Cooperative Education ................................................................. 46

## Part Three: Ready to Apply?

**Chapter 7:** Those Stressful Standardized Tests ................................ 48
  Getting Organized ....................................................................... 48
  Getting Prepped .......................................................................... 49

**Chapter 8:** The Application Form ..................................................... 53
  The Almost-Paperless Application ................................................ 53
  Online Applications ..................................................................... 54
  Get Discovered Before Applying .................................................. 56

**Chapter 9:** Essays, Interviews, and Recommendations ....................... 57

    Ugh! The Essay ............................................................................. 57

    Useful References for Any Writer .................................................. 58

    Don't Forget the Interview ............................................................. 59

    Dealing with Recommendations .................................................... 60

## Part Four: Financial Aid—The Wired Way

**Chapter 10:** Financial-Aid Overview ............................................... 62

    Thinking Ahead ............................................................................. 62

    Financial Aid 101 .......................................................................... 64

    Applying for Financial Aid ........................................................... 66

**Chapter 11:** Federal Student Aid ...................................................... 69

    More on Loans .............................................................................. 70

    Banks, Guaranty Agencies, and More ........................................... 71

    Tax Cuts Explained ....................................................................... 73

**Chapter 12:** Beyond Uncle Sam ....................................................... 75

    State Aid ........................................................................................ 75

    Collegiate Aid ............................................................................... 76

    Focusing on Scholarships .............................................................. 77

    Don't Get Scammed ...................................................................... 80

    Considering the Military ............................................................... 80

    Or Community Service .................................................................. 81

    Aid for Would-be Health Professionals ........................................ 82

    If You're an Athlete ...................................................................... 82

    Recruitment Services ..................................................................... 84

    Commercial Education Loans ........................................................ 84

    Installment Plans .......................................................................... 86

    A Few More Radical Options ........................................................ 86

## Part Five: If You've Procrastinated Too Long ............. 88

## Part Six: Cyber-College Life

**Chapter 13:** The Fun Stuff ................................................................ 90

**Chapter 14:** E-Campus Bookstores and Online Lecture Notes .......... 94

## Appendices

**Appendix 1:** Metasites ...................................................................... 98

**Appendix 2:** FAQs for Internet Newbies .......................................... 104

**Appendix 3:** Index to Every Internet Address in this Book .............. 120

# PREFACE

■ ■ ■ ■ ■ ■ ■ ■ ■ ■ ■ ■ ■ ■

## GETTING STARTED

Consider yourself among the lucky. As a college-bound student, you have
entered the market at a time when the Internet is making the college search,
the application process, and the financial-aid quest easier than ever before.
The World Wide Web is stocked with free (and helpful) directories and
news sources; electronic mail makes it easy to ask questions; and digitiza-
tion is streamlining tasks and eliminating the need for mindless paper
pushing.

But, as many frustrated people have already discovered, the Internet
comes with a major caveat: While good stuff is out there, it can be a
nightmare to find. No one wants to waste an afternoon clicking through
pages of outdated drivel and useless promotions, attempting to download
files that never seem to work, and waiting for oversized color advertisements to etch themselves across the screen.

This book will help you avoid that wasted time. It directs you to Web
sites and online areas with useful information, instead of those that simply
act as indices pointing you elsewhere. (Unless otherwise noted, sites appear
in order of what I consider the most useful.)

- It provides WARNINGS about sites with heavy graphics and programs
  that require additional software and computer memory to run.

- It alerts you to pages you should save as BOOKMARKS or favorites.

- And it offers TIPS to make surfing the Internet, in general, more worth
  your while.

If this is your first time meandering through the Internet, take a few
minutes to read Appendix 2: FAQs for Internet Newbies. It will help you
get your bearings.

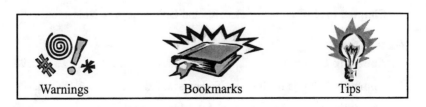

| Warnings | Bookmarks | Tips |

# PART ONE

■■■■■■■■■■■■■■■■■

## Getting Plugged In

# Chapter 1

■■■■■■■■■■■■■■■■■■■

## Site Seeing: The Basics

Consider this the scaled-down, one-stop shop for college-bound students using the Internet. Use this 10-step program as a guide to essential links— or simply as a strategic outline to the chapters that follow.

### Step One—Narrow your list of possible colleges.
nces.ed.gov/ipeds/cool
www.petersons.com
www.collegeboard.com
www.princetonreview.com

### Step Two—Go to their home pages. Learn everything you can about the schools. Bookmark ones you like.
You'll find links to the home pages if you search using the sites from Step One.

### Step Three—Collect objective news and information about the colleges.
www.newslink.org/news.html

### Step Four—Take some virtual tours. E-mail questions along the way.
www.ecampustours.com
Or go to the home pages of the colleges you book-marked. (See Step Two)

### Step Five—Meanwhile, prepare for the SAT or ACT.
www.collegeboard.com
www.act.org

**Step Six—Request, download, or bookmark applications for colleges that interest you.**
Your best bet is to go to the colleges' home pages and head for the online admission office. (See Step Two.)

**Step Seven—Complete your college applications—online if possible.**
www.princetonreview.com
www.applyweb.com
Or, check to see if you can apply directly from your college's admissions page.

**Step Eight—Collect financial-aid information, send in your FAFSA, and register for PROFILE (if necessary).**
www.students.gov
www.fafsa.ed.gov
www.finaid.org
www.collegeboard.com

**Step Nine—Conduct your own scholarship search.**
www.fastWeb.com
www.scholarships.com

**Step Ten—Hang out on the Internet instead of stressing out about acceptances.**
www.collegeclub.com

# Chapter 2

■ ■ ■ ■ ■ ■ ■ ■ ■ ■ ■ ■ ■ ■ ■ ■ ■ ■ ■ ■ ■ ■ ■ ■

## Connecting and Communicating

## Connecting

So, how does the cyber-savvy student get started? The first step is to connect to the Internet using an online service or an Internet service provider.

### Using Internet-service providers

Internet-service providers, or ISPs, offer Internet connections for what is typically a monthly fee. They do not provide content, but they let you go straight to your e-mail account or the Web by opening up a browser like Internet Explorer. Sometimes ISPs have "start pages" (the first screen you see when you log on) with links to popular Web sites and search engines. In your search for college admission information, most of your research will occur on the Web.

Many middle class families are now using high-speed "broadband" ISPs to get connected. Some examples are Cox or Comcast (which offer Internet access via cable) and Verizon (which offers Net access over a special phone line called DSL).

Earthlink, NetZero and Sprint are examples of national ISPs for people who use regular "dial up" phone lines to get on the Internet.

Another option is to get online wirelessly. If you have a laptop equipped with a wireless card you can go to coffee shops and even city parks and find yourself automatically connected to the Internet, sometimes for free. These parks and coffee shops are called WiFi hotspots and they are proliferating around the country,

You'll find local dial-up, DSL/Cable and fixed wireless providers listed at www.thelist.com.

## Using online services

Online services provide subscribers with specialized content, as well as Internet access. Many people use America Online, by far the largest service. Or you might have an account with Microsoft Network (MSN), or ATT.net.

Before you rev up one of these services, however, here are a few pointers:

• When you log in to an online service, you are connected to a large, international network—but you are not necessarily ON the Internet. You may be browsing through the specialized content made available to subscribers of that service only.

• These services will give you direct access to the Web, however. To go directly to the Web, click on an area called "Search the Web" or something similar. Even if you do not go straight to the Web, you might find yourself clicking to a Web page without even realizing it. For example, links to Web pages are embedded throughout AOL. Once you are on these sites you have stepped out of the online service's closed territory and onto the Internet.

• The Internet's unlimited expanse can open up thousands of new sites for you to investigate. If you have a slow computer with a slow modem connection, however, you will sometimes receive information at a slower rate.

• America Online used to limit access to its college area to subscribers only. But now, even without a subscription, you can see the same content. Go to teens.aol.com/college.

# Communicating

Once you successfully connect to an online service or an ISP, you'll be able to communicate with financial-aid and admission professionals, as well as other students across the world. You do this using the World Wide Web, electronic mail, and once in a blue moon, Usenet.

## Using the World Wide Web

Whether you connect to the Internet using an online service or an ISP, you'll find the Web can be slow—especially if you're trying to load a graphics-heavy site and you're not using a high-speed service. When you are looking for college-related information, you may not need to see all of those graphics and would rather receive the text only. You can make this happen by changing the way your browser loads images. (For more information, see the section titled "Why do some sites take so long to load? And what can I do about it?" in Appendix 2.)

If you have access to a computer at your school or library with a faster, more direct Internet connection, use it, especially if you'd like to take some of the graphics-heavy "virtual tours" found on many college home pages.

For more information on the differences between Dial-Up connections (like modems and ISDNs), Dedicated Services (like DSL and Cable), and Wireless ("Wi-Fi"), see Apprendix 2.

## Using e-mail

Even as snazzy graphics, jazzy sounds, and animated images flood the Internet, simple e-mail remains one of its prize attributes. It is quick, convenient, and accessible to folks all over the world, regardless of how advanced their computer systems are. Use it when you can—but be aware of the following as well:

- When you send e-mail to chat rooms and forums, you may unknowingly pass your e-mail address along to companies and individuals who will later send you junk messages you don't want. In fact, Web-based marketing companies are dying to find out your e-mail address. They want the chance to send you unsolicited advertisements, which can quickly clog your mail box. Be careful where you tread. Appendix 2 includes some tips to help reduce junk e-mail.

- Be polite and open in your e-mail messages—especially those you send to admission offices and alumni. Never send just a one-line question like, "Is this a good college?" You'll get no response and annoy the person on the other end. Instead, state your name and where you are from. Ask specific questions. And always say "thank you." It sounds obvious, but it's amazing how many people abandon good manners when shielded by the anonymity of the Internet.

## Using Usenet newsgroups

Usenet (short for "User's Network") represents an older part of the Internet; it's essentially a network of tens of thousands of bulletin boards, or newsgroups, arranged by subject matter. Most newsgroups focus on a single topic, and it's hard to think of something that's not yet covered. (There's even one dedicated to dining hall food called alt.college.food.)

Before the Web became the dominant force of the Internet, these newsgroups were only available to people with "newsreading" or "newsserver" programs, for example, NN Newsreaders (for UNIX machines), and uAccess (for Macintosh machines). Computers in many universities and public libraries still use some sort of newsreader software.

Today, hooking up with a newsgroup is much easier. For example, Google Groups now provides web-based access to all messages posted to Usenet since 1981, archiving more than a billion messages from more than 100,000 discussion groups. The Google folks update this archive several times each day; you can search it from their home page at groups.google.com.

If you want to do more than search you may elect to subscribe to a newsgroup so that you see every message that passes through—and post some of your own. One option is to subscribe through an online service or through a third-party reader such as Mozilla Thunderbird, www.mozilla.org/projects/thunderbird.

But your best bet may be to subscribe via Google and choose to receive (via email) either a daily summary of new posts or the full text. Try groups.google.com/group/soc.college.admissions.

If you decide to subscribe to a newsgroup, and be an active participant (rather than a "lurker"), look through the posted messages for a link to that group's "FAQs" (Frequently Asked Questions). Most newsgroups have their own do's and don'ts, and their members have cruel things to say to rule-breakers.

The newsgroup arena is massive—and hunting for good information is like searching for a needle in a haystack. If you have a specific question, however, feel free to post it to the appropriate newsgroup. You never know what sort of valuable information someone might post in response.

## Using mailing lists

You can also have financial-aid and admission information delivered straight to your e-mail inbox by subscribing to mailing lists that are offered on university web sites. Sometimes lists are designed for admission and financial-aid professionals, and the information can be quite technical. And some organizations restrict their lists to members-only. But keep your eyes open. Subscribe, and you'll be spared the trouble of constantly rechecking for new material.

## One Last Word of Advice

In the razzle-dazzle and convenience of the Internet, don't forget the real world. Talk to the people around you—your parents, friends, siblings, and counselors—about their own experiences in selecting and applying to colleges. Stop by your public library—it's stocked with books that might answer questions the Internet cannot. And visit colleges in person. Nothing beats the experience of physically walking on a campus and talking to the students.

# PART TWO

■■■■■■■■■■■■■■■■■■

## Search, Snoop and Select

# CHAPTER 3

■■■■■■■■■■■■■■■■■■

How can the Internet help you find the perfect college? First, search a variety of online databases to find colleges that fit your interests and visit their home pages to get more detailed information. Next, snoop through college newspapers, and take some virtual tours. Last, select your final choices by gathering impartial information and conducting some interviews of your own.

## Collecting Information About Colleges

The Internet isn't perfect, but one of its major strengths is the ease with which you can search through its vast network of information. Finding a college that meets your criteria is much easier than poring over a 300-page printed directory. Just enter what you want—a small college on the West Coast with an ecology major; a public university with good wheelchair access; or a New England school with study-abroad programs. Then click, and watch the Internet churn out lists of colleges that match.

Several companies design huge Web sites to accommodate this kind of searching. They hope to draw crowds so they can attract advertisers. I call these areas "metasites." In addition to search capabilities, they try to do everything else, too. Some provide how-to articles on getting into college, discussion areas for questions about college essays or campus tours, and financial-aid tips. In most cases, their search engines are their most useful attribute, but they are worth exploring for other information, too.

For a full list of metasites, see Appendix 1. For tips on getting better search results, see Appendix 2.

### COOL's Web search
nces.ed.gov/ipeds/cool

There are three good reasons to visit this site, which is part of a program called College Opportunities Online Locator (COOL). First, it is administered by the National Center for Education Statistics, the federal government's primary agency for collecting current educational data. Second, you can use the search engine without having to register, or reveal any personal data. And third, it allows you to search over 7,000 colleges and universities by geographic region right away, instead of having to select specific states. Once you've selected the criteria that matter most, the matching colleges will appear on your screen. You can then click on the school name to see tuition rates for the past three years. Other useful statistics include average aid awards (including the source of funds), admission data, campus security issues, and enrollment numbers by ethnicity, gender, and attendance status (full-time vs. part-time).

## Peterson's College Search

www.petersons.com

Search through a database that, according to Peterson's, includes every accredited college in the United States and many in Canada. You'll be able to narrow your choice using a variety of criteria, for example: Basics (location, setting, size, cost); Student Body; Academics (degree types and majors); Getting In (selectivity and GPA); and Campus Life (sports, clubs, fraternities and sororities).

After you've received a list of colleges that meet your criteria, you can scan some quick facts about the college, compare it to others you've selected, go to the college's Web site, add information about the college to your personal organizer, or send the college an instant inquiry requesting a catalog, application, or financial aid information. In many cases, you can also click on "Apply" and start filling out the college's application right away. (For more information about online applications, see Chapter 8.)

Like most college search sites, you will need to register with your name, address and email before you can take advantage of all the site's features.

Sometimes you will be faced with a list of things—like states or college names—in a scrolling window on a Web page. To select more than one listing at a time, hold down the Control or Command button on your keyboard when you click on the multiple items you want to include in your search.

## College Board Search

www.collegeboard.com

From the College Board's main page, use "College Quick Finder" to search the College Board's 3,800-school database simply by typing in a college's name. If you're not ready for such specifics, click on "College MatchMaker" to complete a mini-questionnaires about the type of school and campus setting you want. For example, if you search by type of school, you'll be asked whether you seek a private or public college, a single-sex or co-ed college, a historically-black college, and/or a college affiliated with a specific religion. The resulting list will tell you about admission requirements, tuition costs, student life, degrees offered and much more.

If you have already found a school that meets your basic requirements, you can use the "Quick Finder" feature to locate additional colleges with similar features—an easy way to expand your pool of possible colleges.

## The Princeton Review's Counselor-O-Matic

www.princetonreview.com/college

Counselor-O-Matic (from The Princeton Review) asks you about your courses, grades, test scores and extracurriculars, as well as your college preferences—location, size, setting, academics, selectivity, cost, student life, and sports. Then it lets you weigh the importance of these preferences. But you will have to register, providing your e-mail address, to use the search tool.

Many Web sites ask you to register to use their free services. Behind the scenes, these registrations are bartering chips, enabling the site's developers to prove to advertisers that the site has a young, marketable audience. But beware: when you register by typing in your e-mail name and address, you are giving up some of your online privacy. Depending on the company's privacy policy, advertisers will often use that information to find you. You can avoid some of the hassle by keeping your eyes open for registration checkboxes that say things like, "Yes, I would love to receive e-mail messages about new products." If, in fact, you have no desire to receive these veiled advertisements, make sure that the check box is not marked in any way that would imply your permission.

## XAP's Mentor Web Sites

www.xap.com/gotocollege

Use XAP's "College Finder" or "College Matching Wizard" to narrow your search. The interface is clean and friendly.

XAP has also created "Mentor Systems" for over 25 states, including CT Mentor, IllinoisMentor, TexasMentor, NYMentor, and OhioMentor. You can find them using the drop-down menu on the left-hand side of the site. At most of these sites, students can use the "Matching Assistant" to find and rank the best school for them, as well as take virtual campus tours, apply for admission online, and learn about financial aid opportunities. You can link directly to these sites from within XAP. XAP has recently added two additional mentor systems—Christian College Mentor and HBCU Mentor, a guide to Historically Black Colleges and Universities.

## Best College Picks, From Peterson's

www.bestcollegepicks.com

This tool from Peterson's asks you a series of questions about your abilities, goals and values, then matches you to a list of possible colleges based on your responses and those of graduates from those colleges. The results are fun, and interesting, but should be used only in conjunction with other search methods. When we asked a group of college graduates to take the quiz, we were surprised that none of them were matched to their alma maters, especially since they all enjoyed their college experience.

You might want to skip questions about the level of tuition your family is willing (or able) to pay so as not to limit your search unnecessarily. Remember, more expensive colleges often award more generous aid packages, so a $40,000 college may cost you no more out-of-pocket than a $25,000 college.

## CollegeNET

www.collegenet.com

Search through more than 4,000 colleges based on tuition cost, institution type (public, private, or religious affiliation), geographic region, average GPA of freshman class, and intercollegiate sport offerings. CollegeNET retrieves matching colleges quickly—displayed in alphabetical order, but sortable by tuition rate, test scores, enrollment size, ethnicity, or application deadline. By clicking on a college's name, you'll get additional information including a link to the college's home page, an online application, tuition data and details about admissions, financial aid, campus life and academics. CollegeNET also searches databases of information about MBA Programs, vocational/technical schools, and medical or nursing schools.

## Find Your Ideal School, by *U.S. News*
www.usnews.com/usnews/edu/college/tools/search.php

Search the magazine's online directory of nearly 2,000 colleges by name or narrow the field further by using advanced search options like how far away from home you want to be, how much you can afford, selectivity, academic programs and varsity sports programs. To get a full profile of your matches, you must subscribe to *US News'* Premium Online Edition (for $14.95). Otherwise you get just a few tidbits.

Some searchable databases may look complete—even when they are vastly understocked. Some sites only provide information on colleges they have under contract or colleges listed in specific directories. Don't be fooled into thinking these are the only colleges that exist. And never rely on just one data-base, unless you can be sure the information is comprehensive.

Your best bet may be the federal government's searchable data base (COOL), run by the National Center for Education Statistics and mentioned at the beginning of this chapter. It includes 7,000 institutions of higher education in the United States.

## Careers and Colleges
www.careersandcolleges.com

A snazzy look at hundreds of "featured" private colleges (and a few public ones), based on profiles provided by the colleges themselves. In addition, you'll find "Detailed Facts" on over 4,000 two- and four-year colleges. Produced by Alloy Education, the publishers of *Private Colleges & Universities* magazine in association with Wintergreen/Orchard House Press.

## The College Guide
www.mycollegeguide.org

Search by region, cost, freshman-class size, surrounding community size, or school type.

When typing addresses, or URLs, into a Web browser, type exactly what you see—even if it seems something's missing. Some addresses, for example, end in ".htm" and others end in "html". The files with ".htm" endings were probably created on computers that did not allow four-character file extensions. Web browsers read ".htm" files without a problem—but if you type ".html" on a file named ".htm," the browser may give you an error message.

## CollegeView

www.collegeview.com/collegesearch/index.jsp

CollegeView lets you search over 3,800 college profiles by area of study, location, student-body size, religious affiliation, athletic programs, ethnicity, city size, special programs and services for the disabled. You'll receive detailed results for each college—including data on international student and minority student representation. CollegeView also links you to multimedia virtual tours (for its featured schools), complete with audio clips and home page links.

# Looking for Specific Types of Schools

If you want to cut to the chase and search only for information on historically black colleges or Catholic colleges for example, these sites might help. The next section of this chapter, "Finding and using college home pages," offers some options, too.

## HBCU Connect

www.hbcuconnect.com

This nicely revamped site provides a gateway to the HBCU Web—a list of home pages for Historically Black Colleges and Universities—as well as a guide to what issues are facing HBCUs. Includes information and links to employment and scholarship information, online chats, videos and photo albums, and information networks for the African-American community.

## Hillel

www.hillel.org

Hillel, the national organization of Jewish college students, has put together a sharp Web site on student life. Click on "Guide to Jewish Life on Campus" and you'll find links to Hillel chapters at over 500 colleges throughout the world. Learn whether a college provides kosher meals, how many Jewish students are on campus, whether religious services are held on-or off-campus, how many Jewish Studies courses the school offers, whether the school has a "Study in Israel" program, and how active the Jewish student population is.

## The Association of Jesuit Colleges and Universities
www.ajcunet.edu

Nationwide, there are 28 Jesuit Colleges—from Boston College in Massachusetts to Xavier University in Ohio. Use the site's general listing to find one near you, or use the site's search service to seek out the college that offers the major you like in the location you want.

As you register for sites, you will be creating many usernames and passwords. To help you remember them all, store them at PasswordSafe.com.

## Studyabroad.com
www.studyabroad.com

If spending a semester abroad is important to you, do some research on which programs are available through which universities before you apply. This directory will let you search programs in more than 100 countries, and link you to the sponsoring school's home page for more information. This site can also help you find summer study abroad programs, internships abroad and intensive language programs.

## Study Abroad with CIEE
ciee.org/study.aspx

If you're looking specifically for study-abroad programs run by the well-established organization called CIEE, this is your site. For quick searching, go to the "Jump to a Program" function, select either "Teach" or "Study" and then tell the search engine which country you'd like to visit. CIEE administers approximately 95 study abroad programs in over 33 host countries and teaching programs in Chile, China, Spain, and Thailand. It is the leading non-governmental organization for information about international education.

## Collegeabroad.com
www.collegeabroad.com

If you'd rather spend all four years abroad, and earn your degree from an international college or university, you can start your research here. Like its sister-site above, Collegeabroad.com lets you search through full-degree programs worldwide and links you to the sponsoring school's home page for more information.

## Finding and Using College Home Pages

Most colleges have pumped up their Web sites—or home pages—as a way to recruit new students. So be sure to go to the Web pages of colleges that interest you. You'll often find:

- Maps and parking information—print these out before you leave for a campus tour.
- Admission information, including applications to download or complete on line—check deadlines and requirements before you apply.
- Calendars of special events and academic schedules—get a sense of what is offered year-round.
- Press releases—take a peek at the administration's view on what's happened lately, or find out which faculty members are in the news.
- Electronic viewbooks—take a cyber-peek around the college, remembering that professional photographers and copywriters are paid lots of money to make it look and sound good.
- Financial-aid information—find out about special scholarships, payment plans, and application deadlines.
- Student-activity links—get more information on sports and clubs of interest, student services, even the career center's resources.
- Directories—link up with current students, staff, faculty, and alumni. You'll find e-mail addresses, blogs, and personal home pages.
- Links to student newspapers—read students' views on news, academics, and social life.
- Statistics and data—look up graduation rates, sizes of entering classes, and faculty-to-student ratios.
- Invitations to online open houses—meet prospective students in real time over the Net.
- Did I mention the library? Often, you can browse the cyber-stacks.

What you should not do, however, is use these home pages as your sole source of information. Consider much of what you see as a digital brochure. Each college will put itself in the best possible light, hiding all flaws as best it can. Don't be swayed by a sunny photograph of the library when you have yet to see the rest of the campus. On the other hand, don't write off a college just because it doesn't have a snazzy Web site.

The following sites will link you to college home pages. They are listed in order of increasing specificity.

### YAHOO!'s College Listings

dir.yahoo.com/Education/Higher_Education/
Colleges_and_Universities

Yahoo! includes one of the most complete lists of college home pages—including universities around the world. From the link above, you'll get to a page that offers you the option of searching "By Region." Click that to get to home pages for universities in the United States, organized alphabetically by state, or to schools in other countries, organized by country.

### All About College—Search Internationally

www.allaboutcollege.com

This site provides a comprehensive directory of universities around the world. Click on "College Directory," then choose a region in which you'd like to study, and you'll be linked to home pages of that country's schools. The listings for U.S. schools include e-mail addresses for admission offices.

### U.S. Universities and Community Colleges

www.utexas.edu/world/univ

The folks at the University of Texas at Austin regularly update this comprehensive index of links to college home pages. Organized alphabetically or by state, it's an easy, no-frills way to locate your preferred colleges.

### Foundation for Independent Higher Education

www.fihe.org/tools/map.asp

Search tips as well as links to nearly all private universities in the United States, and to organizations in each state that act as advocacy groups for private colleges.

### Canadian Colleges

www.uwaterloo.ca/canu/index.html

Links to all institutional members of the Association of Universities and Colleges of Canada as well as related sites on studying in Canada.

### Community College Web

www.mcli.dist.maricopa.edu/cc

Links to more than 1,285 community colleges in the United States and a dozen other countries, including Canada, Iceland and Indonesia.

## Community College Finder

www.aacc.nche.edu

The American Association of Community Colleges site links you to member institutions and provides statistics, history factoids, lists of outstanding community-college alumni, and a report on the fastest-growing occupations.

## ALLSchools.com

www.allschools.com

Use ALLSchools' career-specific school directories as a quick way to find degree programs by subject matter, for example, ActingSchools.com, EngineeringSchools.com, and WeldingSchools.com.

## Professional and Graduate Schools

www.gradschools.com/search.html

A fairly comprehensive list of graduate school programs—including everything from the basics (like business and law) to more obscure programs (like acupuncture and packaging science). You'll be led to general information about specific universities, as well as links to their home pages and e-mail addresses for their admission offices.

## The Women's College Coalition

www.womenscolleges.org

Links to women's colleges, as well as a history of women's colleges and lists of notable graduates.

## American Indian Higher Education Consortium

www.aihec.org/colleges.cfml

Provides an overview of tribal colleges and links to their home pages, plus a clickable map showing where all 35 are located. For colleges without Web sites, the site offers other contact information.

## Hispanic Association of Colleges and Universities

www.hacu.net

Gateway to over 200 Hispanic-Serving Institutions (HSIs) located in fifteen states and Puerto Rico as well as nearly 120 Associate Members located in eighteen states. To be considered an HSI, 25% of the total enrollment must be Hispanic; for Associate Members, 10% of the total enrollment must be Hispanic. The site also describes a variety of student internships and provides links to numerous scholarship resources.

# CHAPTER 4

■■■■■■■■■■■■■■■■■■■■■

## SNOOPING FOR
## THE REAL STORY

## Getting the Latest College News

Browsing through student newspapers and other online news services is a good way to get a relatively objective view of a college. So snoop around. Is your number-one pick cutting services or raising tuition? Is your state's university opening a new dining hall, computer lab, or football stadium any time soon? Will the campus become a major construction zone for the first three years you are attending?

Before the Internet, these news developments were not always easy to discover—especially if you had not yet visited the campus. But student newspapers have leapt onto the Internet en masse—and many provide archives of back issues, allowing you to gain a better sense of what has been happening on campus all year.

### U-WIRE
www.uwire.com

Read stories and headlines from hundreds of online student papers across the country. Created by journalism students at Northwestern University, UWire is now a subsidiary of CSTV: College Sports Television.

### College News Online
www.collegenews.com

Includes a small but interesting collection of headlines from student newspapers across the country, in addition to fledgling job-search services.

If you already know which colleges you are interested in, you might have the most luck going straight to the college's home page and clicking to the student newspaper. Some colleges make it easy —they link to publications or news straight from their main page. Most of the time, though, you may have to poke around first. Try clicking on sections called "Student Life" or "Student Organizations" or search for the words "student newspaper." Or go to the directories of college papers listed on these pages.

## News Link

newslink.org/statcamp.html

This is a great resource for news publications of any kind—including campus newspapers which are listed here alphabetically by state. Of course, you might find extra nuggets of information by searching through the professional newspapers that cover colleges you are considering. This site provides links to those papers as well, also organized by state.

Most college papers publish only sporadically during the summer, so take time during the school year to browse the online papers of colleges that interest you. To find interesting articles, try searching on words like tuition, arrests, construction, dining, protests.

## Inside Higher Ed

insidehighered.com

Higher education news, commentary, blogs and discussion areas, even a little bit of investigative reporting. It was opened in 2004 by two former editors and a former advertising executive at the *Chronicle of Higher Education* (see below). And as the site sponsors say, the content is all free so everyone can be an insider. The site lists news stories from the past two weeks, and includes a searchable archive for older articles.

## The Chronicle of Higher Education

chronicle.com

If your parents work in education, they might have a subscription to *The Chronicle*. If so, tell them to bookmark this site and get a password (it's free

to subscribers—just send an e-request to member-today@chronicle.com).
Then you'll be able to plug into daily news on anything that affects colleges
and universities. Your high school guidance counselor might have access, as
well. Or, you can subscribe yourself for $80 per year.

But even if you don't have a subscription and password, you can browse
the non-premium articles as well as "Today's News," a free daily blog
highlighting higher education stories from around the web.

### Education News
www.topix.net/education

If you're still searching for that golden nugget, head over to Topix which
gathers information from 50,000 sources and 360,000 user forums around
the world. To narrow the news flood, click on the "local" tab and then
search by the city where your college is located.

### National Association for College Admission Counseling
www.nacacnet.org

High-school counselors might want to take a peek at NACAC's main site.
It is designed for college admissions officers, but also provides information
and forms for those in the secondary-school arena, including an electronic
mailing list, research data and updates on federal issues.

## Getting the Regional Scoop

Check out these sites for details on colleges in the area of the country
you'd like to make your next home. They are listed alphabetically.

### Houston Area Higher Education Resources
www.chron.com/content/community/higher_ed/index.html

*The Houston Chronicle's* directory of college Web sites in the area, plus
links to alumni associations, student organizations, student publications and
more.

If the region you want is not listed here, go to the area's online
newspaper and search using the keywords "college" or "higher
education." Or click on the "community" sections to see
if they have recent news on local colleges. To find the
area's online newspaper, go to Newslink at
newslink.org.

### The New York Times' Education Coverage

www.nytimes.com/pages/education

Serves up daily news about education issues and events, including higher-education coverage. Don't miss the Education Life supplement and technology columns also available on line.

### Los Angeles Times' Education Coverage

www.latimes.com/news/education

Updated daily, this section fills you in on the latest education news to hit the Los Angeles area and beyond.

### The Washington Post's Education Coverage

washingtonpost.com/wp-dyn/education/content/education

Read national news about trends in higher education, converse with college officials in online chats, and find directories to college home pages.

## Thinking About Safety

### Security on Campus, Inc.

www.securityoncampus.org

The mission of Security on Campus, Inc. is to prevent campus crime and violence. This site includes links to campus crime statistics, and information about legal rights and victim assistance programs—important background for all college-bound students.

## What About College Rankings?

Colleges are virtually impossible to rank. There are so many variables—location, mission, size, tuition costs, professor-to-student ratios, you name it. College-bound students should never rely on simple numbered lists to find what they want. But despite the shallowness that results from rankings, various media outlets continue to promote them. Top-10 lists sell, after all. The following publications put their rankings on the Web.

### U.S. News & World Report

www.usnews.com/sections/education

Updated each August, U.S. News & World Report produces some of the most popular and influential lists—even though they are criticized by college officials throughout the country for turning college comparisons into a popularity contest. Take its ratings with a grain of salt. The site is well-designed, however, and full of other useful data, including a couple of less-controversial "Top-100" lists, such as rankings of colleges that have the most students receiving merit-based aid, the most students studying abroad, the most students in fraternities or sororities, or the most students over age 25.

## The Princeton Review's Best 366 Colleges

www.princetonreview.com/college/research/rankings/rankings.asp

Students are the experts here, ranking the country's "Best 366 Colleges." In publishing the survey results, The Princeton Review groups colleges by their top scores in academics, quality of life, politics, demographics, social life, extracurriculars, and parties. This year's best school for overall classroom experience? Reed College. What about the best parties? Top mentions go to West Virginia University, the University of Mississippi, and the University of Texas-Austin.

You can also do a "reverse" search—enter a school's name and see whether students value it for a well-stocked library or a well-stocked bar.

## Maclean's University Rankings

www.macleans.ca/universities

Visit this site to learn how Maclean's Magazine ranks over 47 Canadian colleges. You'll find interesting articles, too. The rankings are posted each November.

## College Ranking Service

www.rankyourcollege.com

This site takes a totally tongue-in-cheek approach to college rankings.

# Thinking Critically

A few companies and colleges have sworn against rankings like those compiled by *U.S. News.* They have created sites and written online essays to describe their reasons, and they strive to provide what they say is a better service.

## College and University Rankings

www.library.uiuc.edu/edx/rankings.htm

Librarians at the University of Illinois at Urbana-Champaign have put together a comprehensive site about college rankings—including references to articles about their validity. See their section on the controversy over rankings for a quick overview on how universities and associations are trying to fight ranking outfits like *U.S. News.*

You'll also find links to several more interesting rankings, like the Mother Jones list of Top Ten Activist Schools, the John Templeton Foundation list of Colleges that Encourage Character Development, and the Campus Squirrel Listings, which equate the quality of a university with the health of its overall squirrel population.

## Student Guide to Evaluating Information
## Technology on Campus

www.educause.edu/StudentGuidetoIT/873

A nonprofit group is now offering an online consumer guide to help students and parents determine what technology matters most on campus. Learn what questions to ask, such as "Are there wireless connections on campus?" "Is technology training available?" and "How will you use technology in your degree program?"

# CHAPTER 5
■■■■■■■■■■■■■■■■■■

## SELECTING THE BEST
## SCHOOLS FOR YOU

Decisions. Decisions. You've seen what's out there, and it's almost more than you can take. You should apply to no more than six colleges; so how will you decide which would be best? First, take some campus tours...in person, if possible. Otherwise, explore the virtual world. Next, gather as much additional advice as you can—from college experts as well as your peers. And finally, do some interviews of your own.

## Preparing For a Campus Tour—
## The Real Thing

The best way to learn about a college is to visit in person, talk to real students, stay in real dorms, sit in on real classes, and eat real dining-hall food. But don't you dare arrive on a campus blind, driving around endlessly looking for parking only to find that the college doesn't give tours on the day you've arrived. You have no excuse now that the Internet exists. Before you take off for a trip, do five things:

1) Read the College Board's collection of articles on planning college visits (www.collegeboard.com/student/csearch/college-visits/index.html). Figure out the best time for you to make your visits, as well as what kind of campus setting you enjoy most—the big city, the 'burbs or the wilds.

2) Go to the home page of the college you are planning to visit. You will probably find those necessary details, such as the hours of operation for the admissions office, the location of the undergraduate library, and how to get to the visitors' parking lot. If you'd like to sit in on a class, browse the course catalog. Jot down classroom numbers and times. Also, take a look at the college's calendar of events. You might want to plan your trip around the Asian-American Student Association's annual bash, or the next home soccer game.

3) At the admissions page, learn whether the college requires on-campus interviews. If you can't tell from the information supplied, look for an admission office e-mail address and send a message asking what is recommended. (See Chapter 9's section on interviews for more information.)

4) Then go to CitySearch (www.citysearch.com) and search using the name of the town you are visiting. If it is a relatively large town, you'll probably at least find a map of the area and a restaurant guide. You might even find a service that gives you hotel rates and tourism tips. After all, if your parents (and/or siblings) plan to join you, you might as well turn the college tour into this year's family vacation.

5) If you're driving, use MapQuest (www.MapQuest.com) to plan your journey. Plug in your home address and your final destination and you'll get door-to-door directions, as well as detailed maps showing each and every turn on the way.

## Taking a Campus Tour—Virtually

These just aren't the same as the real thing. No one disputes that. But taking virtual tours—which are usually similar to watching videos or slow slide shows—can give you a better sense of a campus than staring at a static brochure. If a college offers a virtual tour, it will usually link you to its "campus tour" from the front page or its admission section.

But before you take the plunge, take note:

1) Tours that describe themselves as videos usually require utilities known as "plug-ins," like QuickTime or RealVideo. If you have not updated your Web browsing software — like Internet Explorer or Netscape — in several years, you may have to download and install these plug-ins before the tours will work. (For more information, see Appendix 2.)

If you are using a relatively slow machine, it is not worth your time to even attempt to watch tours that use videos or animation. Save yourself the frustration and go to more useful sites that don't require as much work.

2) Don't take these tours during the Internet's rush hour. Avoid the early evening, when millions of people are taking a look online. Try them in the early morning or late at night to avoid slow-downs. These tours are built around color photographs, which can take longer than other files to appear on your browser.

3) Be prepared to get "stuck" in a virtual tour: You have clicked on the arrows, seen a few photos, and have had your fill. How do you find your way back? If you're using a fairly advanced browser, you should be able to pull down a menu of sites you've visited by dragging on the space where you key in the URL. From there you can select the address you'd like to revisit. If you can't find it, hit the "back" button until you find your way out.

## eCampusTours

www.ecampustours.com

Once you register, you can tour over 1,200 college campuses without leaving home. Take a peak inside dorm rooms, the dining hall, classrooms, labs and the library. Or, visit the athletic facilities and the main quad. When you're finished with your stroll, you can save the tour in a portfolio and contact the admission office for additional information.

## The U

www.theu.com

See video clips hosted by teen TV stars that give you a peek inside college dorms as well as the insights of current students.

## CampusTours.com

www.campustours.com

For a direct route to a college's virtual tour, head to this index. Colleges are listed by state, and alphabetically. Virtual tours offer 360 degree views of everything from student centers to athletic facilities to dorm rooms.

Some of these tours have words like (975K gif) in parentheses next to the links. Pay attention to this information if your computer is slow or old. A GIF is an acronym for a graphic that shows up on the Web. It is derived from the file extension ".gif" (graphics interchange format) that tells the computer the file is a type of compressed image. Another type of graphic is called JPEG (Joint Photographic Experts Group). In general, 975K is a whopping file, while 9K is something every computer should be able to handle quickly.

## Collegiate Choice Walking Tours DVDs

www.collegiatechoice.com

A catalog of in-depth videos based on nearly 400 college campuses, conducted candidly and independently of the colleges themselves. Some videos run for more than an hour providing a view of the college tour as if you were there, walking along with the crowd. It also presents interviews with students on campus. The cost is $15 per video, with $6-10 per order more for shipping.

# Gathering More Advice

If you're not already overwhelmed with advice from your folks, your high-school guidance counselor, your friends, and random junk mail, you might want to take a peek on line. You'll find chat rooms where you can question "experts," forums where you can read people's posts and add your own, plus general advice and time-management tips.

## The College Board's Starting Points for Parents and Students

www.collegeboard.com

The College Board web site lets you choose from three separate paths, "For Students," "For Parents," and "For Educators." Pick a path, then click on tabs like "Plan for College" or "Find a College." Each one offers several useful clusters of essays, including "Senior Action Plan" and "Tips For Finding Your College Match."

## About.Com's College Admission Section

collegeapps.about.com

Read essays full of worthwhile advice, and check the college admissions chats and forums. About.com also takes you to dozens of other college planning sites, many of which are listed in this book.

## College Comparison Worksheet

www.usnews.com/sections/education

Are you still trying to narrow your options? Are there three or four colleges you simply can't choose between? Premium Subscribers to the *U.S. News* site may use this online worksheet to analyze how they differ. It might be smart, however, to apply to several of them anyway—just in case you don't get into the one you thought was a perfect fit.

## College QuickFinder: Compare

apps.collegeboard.com/search/sidebyside.jsp

The College Board site offers free side-by-side college comparisons, however, it displays considerably less data in its comparisons than the fee-based site from US News.

## College Personality Quiz

http://www.usnews.com/usnews/edu/college/articles/extras/personality-quiz_brief.php

If you need to re-examine what you're looking for in a school, you might take the (free) *U.S. News* "College Personality Quiz." You'll find it at this link, or under the "Best Colleges" heading at the main USNews site.

If you come across a site that charges a fee to help you get into school, it is probably not worth the money. Some, in fact, are true scams. With all the free information available—and easily accessible on the Internet—there is little need for such services. Besides, 80% of all students get into their first-choice school; 95% get into one of their top two choices. What about that other 5%? They probably didn't do their webwork, so they applied to colleges that weren't right for them in the first place!

## Dear Admissions Guru . . .

www.mycollegeguide.org/Guru.php

Here you'll find answers to college planning questions provided by a well-meaning Web personality named the Admissions Guru.

## Getting Ready for University

www.campusaccess.com

Although it is aimed at students planning to go to Canadian schools, the "education" section of this site can help students anywhere decide whether to stay close to home or move far away, or whether to choose a small town or head to a larger city. It also includes essays on saying goodbye to high school and getting ready for college.

For more Web sites that offer general advice, see the "metasites" listed in Appendix 1.

### Princeton Review's "Eye on Apply"

www.princetonreview.com/college/apply/eyeonapply/2007/
default.asp

This feature, added in 2006, allows you to look over the shoulders of 11 high school seniors as they go through the admission process. Each of the students has posted information about where they decided to apply, which colleges accepted them and where they eventually chose to go. Their insights may help you to avoid mistakes—like Chloe's admission that she wished she hadn't spent time on applications to schools that she knew she would never attend.

## Do Some "Social Networking"

There's a new—and admittedly addictive—way to find people who are connected to the colleges you like: Seek them on social networking sites like Facebook.com. These sites enable you to post as much or as little information about yourself and then link yourself to people who know you. From there, you find links to people who know those people, who know more people, and so on.

In other words, you can't just find and email perfect strangers. But you just might find a friend of a friend who can give you the straight story about what they think of their college or alma mater. Here are the top social-networking sites in 2007:

Facebook.com

MySpace.com

Xanga.com

Friendster.com

## Using Forums

### U.S. News's College Forums

www.usnews.com/sections/education

Look for "Discussion Community" and click on the "College" forum and you'll find dozens of questions from confused students just like you. U.S. News has pulled together a panel of admission and financial-aid experts to answer your most vexing questions.

## The Princeton Review's Forums

discuss.princetonreview.com

Jump into discussions with other students about choosing a college, the latest movies, college life, help with your high school homework, and nearly everything else. First, you'll have to register. There's also a "parents only" section on surviving the admission process and discussing boards for individual colleges.

 Don't get sucked in. You can waste hours clicking around forums searching for a gem of information, hogging the phone line all afternoon. Meanwhile, you could be exploring useful Web sites.

# Do Some Interviews of Your Own

Finally, and most importantly, don't be afraid to do your own interviewing. In this era of hyper-communication, you have the tools at hand to find professors and students who might be able to answer specific questions. Some admissions offices will provide names of students whom you may contact through e-mail. Give them a try. But you might get a more balanced sense of what people truly think about the college by contacting the students in various organizations or professors in various departments.

How do you find them? First, go to the college's home page. Then, instead of clicking on the admission office link, click on one for "Student Life," "Student Organizations," or something similar. Browse around depending on your interests. Some student unions have developed fairly sophisticated Web pages, which include student e-mail addresses. Send e-mail straight from the Web if you are on your own computer, or jot down their addresses to use later.

The same strategy will work for professors. If you click on a section with a title like "Academic Departments," or "College of Arts and Sciences," you'll eventually come to a list of department pages. Click on those that interest you, and find addresses for professors.

Sending e-mail, especially to professors, does not guarantee a response. They may not have time to respond to queries from students they do not know (or who aren't in one of their classes). You will get the best results if you send personal and targeted e-mail messages with very specific questions.

Don't forget alumni networks, either. Some universities link straight to an alumni section from their home pages. You might get lucky and find some e-mail addresses for recent alums there. Don't hesitate to drop them a note.

Use e-mail etiquette when sending notes to enrolled students and professors. Always state clearly why you are writing, and ask specific, thoughtful questions. Lastly, always sign your name, your e-mail address, and hometown or high school at the bottom of the message. You never know if these are professors or students you will someday meet in class—so make a good impression!

## The Daily Jolt

www.dailyjolt.com

A collection of (unofficial) college web sites created and run by students who actually attend the college. You can get a nice sense of each included school through listings of on- and off-campus events, daily Dining Hall menus, dorm room tours, ride boards, course catalogues, course evaluations, and more. You can also interact with students at the schools through discussion forums and links to student home pages.

To get a full sense of a college, don't limit your "conversations" to a single student or alum. And never let one strange home page color your impression of an entire school.

# CHAPTER 6

■ ■ ■ ■ ■ ■ ■ ■ ■ ■ ■ ■ ■ ■ ■ ■ ■ ■ ■ ■

## CONSIDERING DISTANCE EDUCATION
## AND COOPERATIVE EDUCATION

Today's collegiate environment is changing fast, so even if you're short on cash, short on time, or older than traditional college students, you can still earn a college degree. The two most popular alternatives to the typical four-year degree are distance education and cooperative education.

## Learning About Distance Education

Distance education has become a hot—and hyped—discussion topic in education circles today. Even the most traditional institutions have pulled their heads out of the sand to get involved. If you are looking for a traditional, on-campus experience, chances are the college you select will be offering some online education as well.

If you are looking for a less-traditional experience, you'll have more choices than ever. Single and/or working parents are some of the most common enrollees of Internet-based college programs. Members of the military and students with disabilities, especially, may find distance education an attractive alternative option. But remember these two caveats:

*First*, work smart. Online courses number in the thousands, so make certain you select ones that will earn you credits toward a recognized degree.

*Second*, be careful. The concept of Internet-based education is still so new it can be difficult to sort out the legitimate, worthwhile programs from the rip-offs. For starters, check to see if a program is accredited by a nationally-recognized agency or if it has a relationship with other accredited colleges. Some bricks and mortar colleges find a combination of on-site courses and off-site Net-based courses work best.

## Accreditation

Accreditation is like a stamp of approval—awarded only to educational programs that meet specific standards of quality. Future employers, for example, will need reassurance that you graduated from a legitimate, accredited, institution. Similarly, the federal government reserves its student-aid funds for students attending accredited schools. This chapter explores valuable resources for information on accreditation, plus several online indices to distance-education programs.

## Council for Higher Education Accreditation

www.chea.org

The "Databases and Directories" section of this site is the best resource for determining the legitimacy of an online degree program. It provides a list of accrediting agencies recognized by CHEA and the U.S. Department of Education. If a program is accredited by an unfamiliar agency, you can use these directories to determine whether that agency is, in fact, nationally recognized.

I can't stress enough how important it is to be sure your distance-education program is accredited by an agency recognized by the Department of Education or the Council for Higher Education Accreditation. Seedy Web sites keep cropping up, posing as accredited distance-learning programs. They'll tell you they are accredited, when in reality they have been 'accredited' by a less-than-respectable organization. Don't be fooled into throwing away thousands of dollars on a worthless degree.

## Distance Education and Training Council

www.detc.org

This site is home to the DETC, an information clearinghouse for the distance education field. Founded in 1926, DETC also sponsors a nationally-recognized accrediting agency that evaluates specialized distance-education programs (those with no ties to traditional universities). Go to "Accredited Institutions" and browse the directory of available programs.

## World Wide Learn

www.worldwidelearn.com

This gem of a website features a directory of hundreds of e-learning courses in more than 280 subject areas, as well as helpful articles about accreditation and how to choose the right online program. Based in Canada, this site boasts that it is the "world's largest online directory of education."

## Peterson's Distance Learning

www.petersons.com/distancelearning

Conduct searches for full degree programs or single courses in this comprehensive database. You can even search by keyword. Try "nutrition," for example, and it returns eight schools, complete with in-depth descriptions, contact information and "facts and figures" (including course price tags).

## Yahoo!

degrees.education.yahoo.com

Yahoo's listings now let you narrow your search to online degree programs only. Not every program is listed, but most of the big ones are here, including the University of Phoenix Online and Western Governors University (see below).

## Online School Guide for Online School & Campus Programs

www.directoryofschools.com

This site gets points for helping to organize the overwhelming number of schools that now offer online programs and degrees. Degree listings are sorted by subject (Business, Education, Art, Engineering, Health Care, etc.) and program (Fashion, Marketing, Biomedical, etc.). But the lack of information about the site's founders (not to mention a few spelling and grammar errors) gives me pause. Use it as a first step in gathering information, but be sure to check on accreditation and other standards with other sources, too.

> If you think you may eventually attend a "traditional" college, be sure to ask potential schools whether you can transfer your distance-education credits.

## DANTES

www.dantes.doded.mil

The Defense Activity for Non-Traditional Education Support (DANTES) mission is to support off-duty (voluntary) education programs of the Department of Defense. The DANTES Distance Learning Program is primarily for military personnel whose schedules or duty locations do not permit traditional classroom attendance. The DANTES web site contains a great deal of information on distance learning, as well as a course catalogue of nationally-accredited distance learning degree programs.

### Virtual University Gazette

www.geteducated.com/vug/index.asp

This electronic newsletter is delivered free via e-mail to anyone who wishes to subscribe. Each issue includes a summary of new distance learning programs and links to online learning hot spots. A directory at the Web site features undergraduate and graduate programs that have chosen to advertise.

An overwhelming number of traditional colleges and universities are getting into the e-learning business. In fact, some of the world's most prestigious schools (including Columbia, Stanford, the University of Chicago and the London School of Economics) offer courses online in conjunction with Fathom.com or UNext.com.

Better yet, if you already know which institution you'd like to attend "virtually," go to that institution's home page and search on words like "distance education" or "online courses" to see if it offers such programs.

### Degree.Net

www.degree.net

An appealing site, with news about distance ed and links to useful resources as well as warnings about unscrupulous schools. Degree.Net also includes a searchable data base of distance-learning schools. Much of the site information is based on materials from an original (and irreverent) distance-ed guru named John Bear.

# A Sampling of Distance-Ed Programs

The field of distance education has become so crowded that to list all the available programs would fill another book. But here is a sampling of some of the larger and better-known programs that have arrived on the scene:

### The University of Phoenix Online

www.phoenix.edu

With over 200,000 enrolled students and over 17,000 faculty members, this for-profit university is turning heads throughout the higher-education community. It aims to give working adults a chance to pursue a degree without quitting their jobs or disrupting their schedules. Students attend classes at one of nearly 200 satellite campuses or take distance-education courses. Over 140,000 degree-seeking students study online. The university is fully accredited.

## Western Governors University

www.wgu.edu

Western Governors University—which opened in 1998 with much fanfare but few students—is a collaborative effort among nineteen Western states. The goal is to create an institution to serve working adults by offering them alternative ways to get college-level credentials and learn new skills. Over the past few years, WGU has focused on granting degrees to help professional people switch to careers in teaching, nursing and information technology.

## Capella University

www.capellauniversity.edu

One of the oldest distance-learning schools in the country, Capella offers undergraduate degrees in a variety of topics as well as graduate degrees from schools of Education, Business, Human Services and Psychology. Accredited by the North Central Association of Colleges and Schools, a legitimate group that accredits hundreds of other traditional colleges.

## Jones International University

www.jonesinternational.edu

Jones offers degrees on the undergraduate and graduate level, and holds a cyber-graduation ceremony each year complete with commencement speaker and online reception. "The University of the Web," as Jones once called itself, was the first online university to earn full accreditation—from the North Central Association of Colleges and Schools—triggering concern among traditional educators who weren't convinced that online programs offer the same quality of experience as face-to-face programs. Meanwhile, the number of online courses continues to grow.

## Online Learning at Parkland College

online.parkland.edu

Illinois's Parkland College offers hundreds of online courses as well as a variety of student support services. Click "Online at Parkland" to get information about completing an associate's degree entirely online.

## CIC Course Share

www.cic.net/AcademicCollaboration.shtml

The institutions in the Big 10 Conference (schools like Indiana University and Ohio State) have long worked together to coordinate their academic offerings, and maximize faculty expertise. Now, they have expanded their efforts to include distance-ed courses that can be taken by students at any school within the program.

## The New School Online University

online.newschool.edu

The New School has always looked for alternative ways to provide liberal-arts education, and the school's cybercampus provides yet another. Undergraduates can earn liberal-arts degrees over the Internet. There are dozens of non-degree online course options as well. The school is accredited by the Middle States Association of Colleges and Secondary Schools.

## Servicemembers Opportunity Colleges

www.soc.aascu.org

A consortium of approximately 1800 colleges that provide educational opportunities for servicemembers and their families, and help them earn college degrees, either on-campus, or on-line.

## Southern Regional Electronic Campus

www.electroniccampus.org

An online "campus" providing courses and degree programs from scores of colleges and universities across the South. Take a peek at the current offerings or search for specific courses and degree programs.

## SUNY Learning Network

sln.suny.edu

The State University of New York includes more than 40 campuses—but even if you cannot find a way to physically get to one of them, you still have a shot using the university's Learning Network. Its Web site offers a lot of information to help you get started, as well as a list of 100 online degree programs and 4,300 online course offerings.

# Cooperative Education

Many universities offer cooperative education programs, which enable students to alternate between periods of studying on campus and working, for a salary, at a job related to their career interests. Co-op programs can be an invaluable way to learn skills and earn money for school at the same time. Search the Web sites of colleges that interest you, using words like "co-op" and "cooperative education." Also, Yahoo! and other search engines provide dozens of links to colleges' co-op programs.

## National Commission for Cooperative Education
www.northeastern.edu/co-op

A good starting point for information on cooperative education. Includes illustrations of how Co-op works, as well as an online guide, about the benefits of Co-op called "The Best of Co-op."

## Cooperative Education and Internship Association
www.ceiainc.org

Make this your first stop to get an overview of co-op education. You'll find general information, online resources, and links to other co-op sites including state and regional co-op agencies.

## The Co-op Student Handbook
www.northeastern.edu/coop

Click on "Cooperative Education" to read Northeastern University's terrific online guide for students interested in exploring co-op.

## Studentjobs.gov
www.studentjobs.gov

The federal government also sponsors cooperative education, with Uncle himself serving as the students' employer. This site, developed by the Office of Personnel Management (OPM), has pulled together information on federal co-op, as well as listings of government fellowships, grants, internships, and scholarships  The site even helps students create a winning profile and resume.

# PART THREE

■■■■■■■■■■■■■■■■■■■■■■■

## Ready to Apply?

# CHAPTER 7

■■■■■■■■■■■■■■■■■■■

## THOSE STRESSFUL
## STANDARDIZED TESTS

## Getting Organized

Two tests strike fear into the hearts of most college-bound juniors and seniors: The SAT (which once stood for Scholastic Aptitude Test, then Scholastic Assessment Test, but now is just called the SAT) and the ACT (which once stood for American College Testing). Advanced Placement exams are no fun either. But by tapping into a variety of online resources, you can at least prepare yourself for the worst. For general information and registration forms, check the following sites.

### About the SAT

www.collegeboard.com/student/testing/sat/about.html

The College Board offers students an overview of SAT Subject Tests and the SAT Reasoning Test, including samples of the questions and essay topics. This site also includes an index of useful SAT-related tools. For example, from here you can view and send your test scores and link to the College Board's official "Snack Policy for Test Day."

### SAT Dates and Fees

www.collegeboard.com/student/testing/sat/calenfees.html

The College Board provides a chart with SAT registration deadlines and testing dates for the upcoming year. You'll also learn about test fees and fee waivers (for students from low-income families).

### Online SAT Registration

www.collegeboard.com/student/testing/sat/reg.html

If you plan to pay for the SAT by credit card, and don't qualify for any special waivers, here's a hassle-free way to register and print your SAT "Admission Ticket."

### Educational Testing Service Network

www.ets.org

The Educational Testing Service (ETS) develops the SAT (among other tests) which is then administered by the College Board, a client of ETS. Its site includes sections for students, parents and educators, press releases, practice test questions, and lots of cross links to the College Board. A few years ago, when ETS found a flaw in a test question, the service posted an announcement here about how the error affected test-takers.

### ACT's Web site

www.actstudent.org

This is the electronic gateway to information about the ACT, a competitor to the SAT. It offers test strategies and sample questions, as well as links to electronic college search and application sites.

### ACT Assessment Test Dates

www.actstudent.org/regist/currentdates.html

Test dates, through June, 2008, plus information on when to take the test if you live outside the 50 states.

### Registering for the ACT

www.actstudent.org/regist

Find links for online registration, telephone registration for repeat test-takers, standby testing information, a list of upcoming test dates and deadlines, and the locations of test centers near you.

## Getting Prepped

Reduce your stress level a notch or two by reviewing vocabulary or taking some practice tests. The "Big Three" of test prep have SAT news and SAT tips: The Princeton Review (www.princetonreview), Kaplan (www.kaptest.com) and Peterson's (www.petersons.com). But there are many other useful sites as well.

### Wordsmyth S.A.T. Dictionary

www.lightlink.com/bobp/wedt/sat.htm

A downloadable list of 2000 words and definitions that often appear on SATs. Words with asterisks appear the most frequently, based on a ten-year analysis of SAT tests. Use this to create your own flash-card sessions. Check out the site's "words of the week" and word-game contests, too.

### Number2.com
www.number2.com

This free test-prep service says it automatically adapts to your skill level and provides immediate feedback on every incorrect answer. Prep quizzes are available for SAT, ACT and GRE. The site also offers a "word of the day" and an online "coaching system" for parents, counselors, or testing tutors. Brought to you by XAP.com, the company that creates online state-based college admission portals.

### Kaplan's Test Prep
www.kaptest.com

Kaplan, one of the biggest names in the test-prep business, requires you to register for this site. But once you've done so, Kaplan provides you with a free practice SAT and strategy sessions. Naturally, you can also buy books and sign up for pricey courses. Kaplan charges $399 for its online SAT prep course, and $899 for its in-person, classroom course. Or, you can pay $14.97 and get three separate SAT Prep programs for your iPod.

Kaplan also has a free online option, the SAT QuizBank (formerly this option cost $199). QuizBank includes over 1,000 SAT questions and lets you design your own quizzes by subject, difficulty and length. Kaplan says QuizBank is especially good if you have only a few days to prep before the exam, or you just need help on a specific section of the exam.

### Peterson's Test Prep
www.petersons.com

Peterson's lets you take three practice tests (for as little as $19.95) as well as an affordable ($119-$209) online SAT Prep course. You start by taking a diagnostic exam to assess your core skills, and then proceed through a course which has been tailored to meet your specific needs.

### The Princeton Review
www.princetonreview.com/college/testPrep

If you're just browsing, check the free articles on raising test scores and the in-depth reports on past tests. If you're willing to stick around, register your e-mail address and other contact information and you'll be able to take a free practice exam. And if you're already paying big bucks to take a Princeton Review course, plug in your password to get to more advanced online services. You can also take on online course for $99 - $2,000, depending on how much "live" online assistance you want.

## College Power Prep
www.powerprep.com

More free SAT or ACT help, via the Laboratory and Tip of the Day.

## The Study Hall
www.studyhall.com

The Study Hall features a free SAT improvement course as well as a $10/year premium service called Beat the SAT in 24 Hours (www.beatthesatin24hours.com). The premium service includes a more extensive SAT program including a mystery novella packed with SAT vocabulary words. It's not great literature, and its certainly not what people mean when they tell you, "The best way to prepare for the SAT is to read the classics," but it's a reasonably painless way to absorb some new vocabulary.

## The College Board's SAT Preparation Center
www.collegeboard.com/student/testing/sat/prep_one/prep_one.html

The College Board used to claim the test wasn't coachable. Now it lets you take a free practice SAT to determine where you need the most help, and will (happily) sell you an online SAT review course for $69.95.

## APEX Learning—Online Courses for Advanced Placement Exams
www.apexlearning.com

It used to be that only kids at huge, well-to-do high schools were offered an array of Advanced Placement (AP) courses. Now students anywhere in the country can take them online with several caveats. First, the student needs to have a local mentor, which in most cases means the student needs to work with what the local school district offers. Second, students must have Internet access and the ability to pay the tuition, unless the tab is picked up by the school.

APEX Learning's online courses are taught by trained AP teachers. If you enroll, be prepared to spend about 10-15 hours a week completing multimedia tutorials, reading study guides, and participating in online discussions. Students who sign up for these courses have to be dedicated and self-motivating. Many students choose to take the courses in the summer, when their schedules are not quite so packed.

APEX also partners with The Princeton Review to offer AP Exam review for just $49 per subject. The review includes diagnostic assessments and unlimited access to the company's exam review site.

## AP Help from The College Board

www.collegeboard.com/student/testing/ap/about.html

You can also get AP exam help from the College Board. This site includes an online newsletter, exam information, sample tests and extensive lists of online resources that you can use for further study.

There are 37 AP exams in 22 subject areas. If you are very knowledgeable in a subject area (for example, a foreign language) do some prep work and give it a try. You might earn yourself some college credit. Remember, you don't need to have taken an AP course in order to take an AP Exam.

## AP Credit Policy Info

apps.collegeboard.com/apcreditpolicy/index.jsp

Learn whether a college gives credit and/or advanced standing to students who take AP Exams. In many cases, the answer will vary depending on the test score and subject matter.

# CHAPTER 8

■■■■■■■■■■■■■■■■■■■

## THE APPLICATION FORM

## The Almost-Paperless Application

Everyone complains about applying to college, usually for two good reasons: Using a typewriter to fill out the applications is a real pain, and college essays always invite major writer's block.

Well, that writer's block will probably stick around, but thankfully the days of typing applications are nearly over. The Internet now lets you complete your applications online. Instead of spending time messing with typewriter ribbon and aligning forms to type on the dotted line, you can use that time to think more carefully about what you want to include on the forms in the first place. And in some cases, you won't even have to type your name, address, and social-security number over and over again—the online programs remember the information and fill it in for you.

Paperless applications are becoming more and more prevalent, especially at large state or private universities. In fact, many colleges now encourage students to use the Internet, instead of sending in paper—it's less work for them. Soon, some colleges may only accept online applications.

And here's another bonus: The most advanced systems are now error-proof—the computer program won't accept an entry unless it's filled in correctly. Many colleges have also sprung for online systems that include request forms, Web-based applications, and the ability to check back, using the Internet, to see if you have been accepted.

## Some Caveats

Several caveats remain, however. Here are a few:

- If you don't want to use a credit card, you may have to send a check for the cost of the application through the U.S. mail.
- Some application systems allow you to download application forms electronically but do not yet accept applications that are sent on line. You must print and mail them.

- The ease of the Internet can cause carelessness. Don't hit the "submit" button until you are absolutely sure the application is in perfect shape. Get your parents or counselors to look over your forms before you zap them into the admissions office's inbox. And never send in an essay without having someone else proofread it first.

If you don't have a high-speed connection, be prepared for a long download time. I wouldn't try this during Internet rush hour (which is usually early evenings and weekend afternoons), because you might end up with a half-hour wait. For more help with downloading, see Appendix 2.

## Online Applications

With Web-based forms, applications can truly be completed on line—you don't need paper, printers, or diskettes. Simply register, enter the data, and hit the "send" button.

College admission offices have been scrambling over the past few years to bring you this option and they now advertise them prominently on their admission Web pages. *Go to those pages first.* You'll probably find scads of helpful information—like deadlines and application guidelines—that will make the online application process a lot easier.

To get to a college's admission pages, go to a school's Web site, and look for areas called "Admissions," "Apply," or "For Prospective Students." If you don't see those, try searching on the word "admission." Colleges that cannot yet accept electronic applications may at least offer an electronic way to request the application forms, so that you can receive them via the U.S. Post Office.

If you are visiting a college Web site that doesn't mention online applications, however, you still have some semi-paperless options. First, the college might offer *electronic* applications—application forms that you download to your computer. In most cases, you can fill them out using word-processing programs or they come with their own word-processing software. In rare cases, you must still print them out and then fill them in the old-fashioned way.

Second, a smattering of rival companies have created electronic applications that could be used to apply to the colleges of your choice. Here are some of the biggies:

## CollegeNET's ApplyWeb

www.applyweb.com

Over 400 colleges have signed up to create their online undergraduate applications through ApplyWeb. You must first open an account to gain access to the applications, and CollegeNET warns that your chosen "User Name" will become part of your ID when you transmit your applications to the colleges. The lesson? Don't get too cutesy with your name selection.

Save. Save. Save. Completing your work on a computer is always a risky proposition. The electricity might flicker or your little brother could yank out the phone line. Either way, the stress of applying to college is bad enough without the threat of a digital catastrophe. Many online forms offer buttons that enable you to save your work as you go, or save your work and come back to it later. Use them.

## XAP Applications

www.xap.com/Apply

XAP lets you apply to over 700 different colleges. As you finish each screen of an application, XAP checks your data for errors, omissions and inconsistencies, and saves your work as you go.

## College Board Online

www.collegeboard.com/student/apply

The College Board's online application service lets you personalize "My Organizer" to help you organize and prepare your college applications. It comes complete with checklists to keep you on track. You can work from any computer—in progress applications are saved after each session.

## The Common Application

app.commonapp.org

The Common Application was developed so students would not have to fill out different applications for every school on their list. Instead, they complete this application once and send copies to participating colleges (although some schools require extra information, like an additional essay, supplemental activities sheets or answers to a few extra questions). If you are applying to one of these 315 colleges, you will find an online version of the application at this site, as well as links to these supplemental forms.

## Universal College Application
www.universalcollegeapp.com

The Common Application isn't the only game in town anymore. In 2007, the Universal College Application opened its online doors. So far it covers far fewer colleges than the common app (27 institutions were members at last check, versus the 315 of its rival), but there are some big names among the founding few, including Duke and Harvard. One big distinction between the two services is that the well-established Common Application requires its universities to require essays from their applicants. The new UCA, as it is known in shorthand, does not. That doesn't mean you won't be writing essays. Most of the universities who use the UCA ask for them anyway.

How do you choose between these two services? First, make sure the schools you want are on their lists. Then talk to your guidance counselor and listen for complaints or kudos about which company has the better technology and customer service. Of course, if your college has its own application, you might use it instead, even if the school says it accepts a generic form. Your willingness to complete a unique application indicates greater interest in the college. And with competitive admissions, you want to gain every advantage possible.

# Get Discovered *Before* Applying

Until recently, sending in an application was the only way to capture the interest of a college admission officer. Now, with the advent of online portfolios and new communications Web sites, there is another way. Here is one site—perhaps the first of many—that lets students gain the attention of admission officers around the country.

## Zinch
www.zinch.com

The slogan at Zinch is "Show them you are more than your SAT score. Tell your story." This is an online platform that you control. You decide whether to include your grades and SAT in your profile. You decide how you'd like to be described. The more positives you divulge, the higher the chance that you might get noticed. Zinch's system allows students to "shout out" to universities that interest them, sending notices to admission officers about portfolios that may be worth checking out. It also allows admission officers to search the Zinch database, tracking down students who might make a good match, and sending them messages asking them to apply.

# Chapter 9
■ ■ ■ ■ ■ ■ ■ ■ ■ ■ ■ ■ ■ ■ ■ ■ ■ ■ ■ ■

## Essays, Interviews and Recommendations

## Ugh! The Essay

There is no easy way out of writing that personal essay, but some Internet tools can make your task a little less painful. Just be careful how you use them. Colleges are becoming increasingly wary over the proliferation of essay-writing "help" and online cheating. Duke applications, for example, now make the following request: "We recognize that all good writers seek feedback, advice, or editing before sending off an essay. When your essay is complete, please answer the following: 'Whose advice did you seek for help with your answer? Was s/he helpful? What help did s/he provide?'"

### IvyEssays
www.ivyessays.com

IvyEssays provides—for a fee—editing services and copies of admission essays written by students who got into top colleges. But IvyEssays offers quite a bit of useful free advice, as well, to help you brainstorm your way to strong essay topics, create a variety of structured outlines, develop catchy lead in sentences, and hold your reader's attention until the end. Just for laughs, and reassurance, you should also read the section about funny mistakes that people have let slip into their masterpieces.

To hep reassure the skeptics, IvyEssays promises to work with admission officials who feel an applicant has misused resources from this site.

### EssayEdge
www.essayedge.com

Online tips and quizzes to help you think about your accomplishments, select strong essay topics, and write excellent essays. Sample critiques may spark your own ideas for sharp editing. The free "Essay Help Course" contains six lessons to take you through the whole process: (1) Preparation; (2) Question-Specific Strategies; (3) Essay Structure; (4) Style and Tone; (5) Introductions and Conclusiosns; and (6) Editing and

Revising. Of course, like other essay-service sites, the editors at EssayEdge would be happy to help you polish your final product ... for a fee.

Creators of these commercial essay sites say they are simply showing students what it takes to write their own successful essays and emphasize the evils (and illegality) of plagiarism. Admission officers and others say, "au contraire," and think this can be a gateway to plagiarism. Plus, they are starting to get savvy. If you simply re-use an essay from these sites, chances are the admission officers have seen it already and they'll reject you outright. If you want to shell out cash for these services, use them honestly.

### Cambridge Essay Service
www.hbsguru.com

This site is mostly geared to those poor saps willing to spend $150 - $600 to get help writing their essays. I'd suggest skipping anything with a price tag and heading for the free stuff—"Seven Great Tips" on writing a good essay.

## Useful References For Any Writer

### The Wordsmyth Educational Dictionary-Thesaurus
www.wordsmyth.net

Unsure of a word's spelling? Confused about a word's meaning? This new online dictionary is a quick way to find answers. Plus, it offers synonyms for all its entries. For puzzle addicts, this site also includes a nifty crossword-puzzle helper and an anagram solver.

### Thesaurus.com and Dictionary.com
www.thesaurus.com and www.dictionary.com

You can't beat these sites for their easy-to-remember Web addresses and easy-to-use features. For example, the online version of Roget's Thesaurus lets you type a word similar to the one evading you, and see what pops up. They are both great resources for daily crosswords and word puzzles too.

## The Slot

www.theslot.com

Tongue-in-cheek grammar tips from Bill Walsh, a very witty (and opinionated) copy editor at *The Washington Post,* and author of *The Elephants of Style.* The Slot covers word choice, punctuation, quotations, capitalization, spelling, style and more.

## The Elements of Style

www.bartleby.com

This site provides an online version of the first edition of this writing classic, by William Strunk, Jr. (To find it, select "Strunk's Style" under the list of references.) It's a must read before starting any big writing assignment like your college essays. Learn how to use the active voice, omit needless words, avoid commonly misspelled words, and more.

Bartleby's also includes the full texts of nearly a hundred other classic references, including *Robert's Rules of Order, Emily Post on Etiquette, Gray's Anatomy, The* (King James) *Bible, Bartlett's Quotations, Bullfinch's Mythology, The Columbia Encyclopedia*, and the 18-volume *Cambridge History of English and American Literature.*

# Don't Forget the Interview...

Even in this electronic era, the face-to-face interview holds weight at some schools. The admissions pages of most colleges will tell you whether an interview is required or suggested. If an admissions office offers an e-mail address on its Web page, feel free to send a note asking about scheduling one. Then, make it the last stop on your campus tour.

## The Princeton Review's Interview Advice

www.princetonreview.com/college/research/articleIndex.asp

Under "Advice" you will find a series of feature articles on the admissions process, including the interview. Click there and tap into some smart advice, including essays on what to wear, and what NOT to talk about.

## College Admission Office E-Mail Addresses

www.college-scholarships.com

Scroll down to "Colleges by State." Schools are listed alphabetically (by state) with clickable icons for their admission (and financial-aid) offices.

If you are not working at your own computer, be careful about sending e-mail messages directly from Web sites (unless they are the site of your personal inboxes, like Hotmail or Yahoo). Here's why: Web browsers are usually set to a specific e-mail address—in this case, not your own. Let's say you send a message from a computer at cyberbar@state.com. The recipient is likely to "reply to sender." That reply will go straight to cyberbar@state.com, and you may never know whether you received a response. A good rule of thumb, whether writing e-mails from home or elsewhere, is to sign messages with your e-mail address as well as your name. That way, message recipients will know how to get in touch.

# Dealing with Recommendations

Few online applications are sophisticated enough to handle online recommendations. Your best bet is to follow the directions on the application itself—whether it is electronic or in print. You may want to ask, however, whether the admission office will take recommendations via e-mail. If the person writing the letter is comfortable with e-mail—and the office receiving the letter is also comfortable with the idea—then it may be easier for everyone involved.

## The Secondary School Report Form

www.nacacnet.org/MemberPortal/products/forms.html

This form, at least, is available online. It's for high-school guidance counselors only and must carry the high school's official seal once it is printed and filled out. The form is usually attached to the student's admission application before it is sent.

## The Princeton Review's Advice on Recommendations

www.princetonreview.com/college/research/articleIndex.asp

Under "Advice," scroll to the "Apply" section and you will find a couple of good articles on how to get good recommendations, as well as advice on what to do if your recommenders have yet to recommend you.

# PART FOUR

■■■■■■■■■■■■■■■■■■■

## Financial Aid—The Wired Way

# CHAPTER 10

■ ■ ■ ■ ■ ■ ■ ■ ■ ■ ■ ■ ■ ■ ■ ■ ■ ■ ■ ■ ■

## FINANCIAL-AID OVERVIEW

You've heard the horror stories. Tuition costs are rising at twice the rate of inflation, and students and parents are buckling down for decades of debt. But don't let the hype keep you from finding a way to make college affordable. Beyond the extremes of $40,000 price tags and impossible loan burdens (neither of which are as common as you think) you will find plenty of reasonably priced colleges, low-interest loans, and some shots at scholarships.

Several Internet sites make the financial-aid process much easier. You'll find everything from federal student-aid applications to advice on saving tuition money.

## Thinking Ahead

Get in financial-planning mode, but don't worry about digging around for a calculator. Many Web sites now provide online calculators and other interactive devices that crunch the numbers for you.

### Kiplinger.com

www.kiplinger.com

This site, produced by the personal-finance magazine, offers several worthwhile areas. First, go to "College" (under "Tools and Calculators"), and look for "What will it take to save for a college education?" You'll get a sophisticated tool that tells you (1) how much you'll need to sock away now to reach your college savings goal, or (2) what you'll need to change about your current plan to keep pace with rising college prices (e.g., increase your monthly investment by $75).

Then, under "Your Money," look for "College and Family" to read articles that have appeared in the print version of *Kiplinger's* magazine over the past few years. You'll also find *Kiplinger's* rankings of the best values in public and private colleges and the best "Section 529" college savings plan for your family.

## Money 101 — Saving for College
money.cnn.com/pf/101/lessons/11

Test your financial savvy when it comes to saving for your children's college education. *Money Magazine's* "Saving for College" lesson includes numerous background articles and a quiz that will put you in the mindset. For more information, type "colleges" into the site's search box and retrieve articles, online calculators, and databases.

## Smart Money Magazine
www.smartmoney.com/college

The College Planning section of *Smart Money's* personal finance site includes long- and short-term savings strategies, recommended portfolios (based on the student's expected enrollment date), "529 Plan" calculators and much more.

## Financial Aid Calculators
www.finaid.org/calculators

Mark Kantrowitz, developer of the enormously useful FinAid page described in the next section, has designed nearly 50 free calculators for you to use on line (as well as links to dozens more). For example, *College Cost Projector* estimates how much college will cost in the future. *Savings Growth Projector* shows how your current investment fund will do. *Savings Plan Designer* suggests how much you should save each month to pay your college bills.

*Student Loan Advisor* helps you determine how much you'll be able to repay each month (based on the kind of job you're seeking). *Loan Analyzer* lets you see which loan is "the best deal."

And the *Streamlined EFC Calculator* previews how much Uncle Sam will expect your family to contribute to college costs.

Parents: Don't let results from overly simplistic "How Much You Need to Save" calculators scare you off. They were popularized by greedy investment companies which are all-too-happy to take your money and manage it for you. Remember, you don't pay 100% of a four-year college bill the day your student enrolls. The bills are spread out over four years, so make sure your calculator reflects this longer time-line. Also, you can supplement your savings with a contribution from income and a small loan. A more realistic goal would be to save enough to cover half your expected college costs.

## The College Board's Financial Aid Services

www.collegeboard.com/student/pay

A good overview of savings options as well as a realistic look at what colleges actually cost (most people overestimate the expense) and calculators to help you determine your parents' capacity to take on additional debt, how much your college savings will grow over time, and more.

## Investment Advice

Fidelity (www.fidelity.com)
Morningstar (www.morningstar.com)
Vanguard (www.vanguard.com)
The Street (www.thestreet.com)
Quicken (www.quicken.com)
The Motley Fool (www.fool.com)

Most mutual fund companies, as well as the major investment sites, also provide planning tools for people trying to pay for college. If you have several years before tuition bills are due, you might take a peek at the college planning sections of the sites above.

# Financial Aid 101

There is more than $150 billion available in student aid and education tax credits, most of which comes from Uncle Sam. The rest comes from your home state, your college, your employer, your parents' employer, and a small percent from private scholarships. And how do you get all this aid? Apply. Apply. Apply.

As you wander through the net you will see several offers for free money, scholarships, and—yes—scams. So before you get caught up in that stuff, head for . . .

## FinAid! The Smart Student's Guide to Financial Aid

www.finaid.org

This site is brimming with valuable stuff—updates on just-released reports, answers to frequently asked questions, calculators for determining costs, and links to most aid resources (federal, state, collegiate, and private). Published by Mark Kantrowitz, a computer scientist and author with a wealth of knowledge on the subject, it looks at financial aid from the students' and parents' points of view.

## Students.Gov
www.students.gov

This site was designed to be a 24/7 "student gateway to the US government." Its collection of sites helps students find a job (or internship), e-file taxes, get a passport, register to vote, and plan and pay for a college education. Link to electronic applications, loan information, and financial aid opportunities organized by state.

## College Is Possible
www.collegeispossible.org

This site is part of the response to a major study showing how mis-informed most people are about college costs and the availability of financial aid. The resource section is divided into three main parts: (1) Preparing for College; (2) Choosing the Right College; and (3) Paying for College. The site is sponsored by the American Council on Education and its partner organizations, and is intended to disabuse families of all their misconceptions about college.

Many computers come with Adobe Acrobat Reader pre-installed, but if yours doesn't, you can download the software for free. Go to www.adobe.com for more information, or find help in Appendix 2.

## College Answer, From Sallie Mae
www.collegeanswer.com

This site touches on myriad topics, and is brought to you by Sallie Mae, the huge student-loan company. Read about various financing options including how the loan process works, how to pick a lender and how to borrow responsibly.

## Mapping Your Future
www.mapping-your-future.org/paying

Sponsored by a group of more than 30 state loan agencies who guarantee Federal Family Education Loans against default, this site provides all sorts of college and career advice (in English and in Spanish) to parents, students, and those who already have loans.

To get in touch with the loan agency in your state, go to mapping-your-future.org/about/sponsors.cfm, where you'll find links to their Web pages, organized alphabetically. Here are a few that are especially rich in information:

### California Student Aid Commission
www.csac.ca.gov
www.edfund.org

### Illinois Student Assistance Commission
www.collegezone.org

### Texas Guarantee Student Loan Corporation
www.tgslc.org
www.AdventuresinEducation.org

# Applying for Financial Aid

The only way to get federal-, state- or collegiate-based financial aid is to apply for it. In all instances, you'll need to complete a Free Application for Federal Student Aid (FAFSA). If you've set your sights on an expensive private school, you'll probably have to complete the College Board's PROFILE, as well. In completing these applications, you enable the school's financial aid administrator to learn how much your family can contribute to college costs, and how much you will need in financial aid.

If possible, request a PIN from the Department of Education (www.pin.ed.gov) and complete your FAFSA on line. Not only will your application get processed faster, but internal edits will cut down on mistakes. If your parents are required to sign the FAFSA, they will need their own (separate) PIN.

## Expected Family Contribution
www.collegeboard.com/student/pay

Under "Calculators," the College Board allows you to estimate your "Expected Family Contribution" using the Federal Methodology and the Institutional Methodology to learn (in advance) what the federal government and others think you can reasonably pay, out of your own pocket, toward college costs each year. The Federal Methodology is actually set by Uncle Sam, so assuming you plug in the same family income and asset data, your result SHOULD be the same, regardless of whether you use the College Board's version, or one sponsored by a lending institution (see below). The Institutional Methodology is a more comprehensive formula developed by The College Board (with input from the colleges) to determine your eligibility for non-federal aid, for example, collegiate scholarships.

The Federal Methodology is applied to income and asset data you submit on the FAFSA. (More information on federal financial aid is available in the next chapter.) The Institutional Methodology is applied to income and asset data you submit on the PROFILE (or a college's own aid application).

## FAFSA on the Web

www.fafsa.ed.gov

You can still find paper FAFSAs (usually in your high school guidance office or college financial aid office), but most people now use this electronic version. To complete the application online, make sure your Web browser is Netscape Navigator 6.2 or above, or Microsoft Internet Explorer 5.0 or above.

When you're finished, you can either print and mail a separate signature page or use your "Personal Identification Number" (PIN) to verify your identity (and, later, check on the status of your aid application).

Make sure to save a personal copy of your FAFSA—a step often forgotten by people who fill forms out on line. But don't use the save function listed under your Web browser's pull-down menu—you'll be saving an unprotected (i.e., unencrypted) copy that someone could use to view your personal information. Instead, use the save buttons at the bottom of each screen.

## Fafsa-4-Caster

www.fafsa4caster.ed.gov

Use this tool to get an early estimate of your eligibility for federal student aid, and when you're ready to apply, simply transfer your data from here to to FAFSA on the Web.

Don't be confused by www.FAFSA.com. This enterprising financial aid consultant nabbed a prime domain name, but charges families $49.99 - $189.99 to complete the forms. You can do it yourself for free. Your choice.

## PROFILE

profileonline.collegeboard.com

Many schools and scholarship programs require additional information about your family's finances to help them award non-federal aid. They sign contracts with the College Scholarship Service (the financial-aid division of the College Board) to gather this data via PROFILE. Through this site you can register for PROFILE and fill the forms out online. To complete these Web-based forms, however, you must be running an advanced Web browser.

Ask your parents to start work on their 2007 taxes as soon as possible. Not only will it be much easier to complete the FAFSA and PROFILE, but their income data on all these forms must match pretty closely. The 2008-2009 PROFILE will be available on October 1, 2007; the 2008-2009 FAFSA will not be available until January 1, 2008.

# CHAPTER 11

## ■■■■■■■■■■■■■■■■■■■■■■■■

### FEDERAL STUDENT AID

Pell Grants, Supplemental Educational Opportunity Grants, Work-Study, Stafford Loans, PLUS Loans, Perkins Loans. Through these six gigantic programs, Uncle Sam funds over $60 billion in student aid every year.

## Funding Education Beyond High School: The Guide to Federal Student Aid

studentaid.ed.gov

This site is a must. And from it, you can download a free 60-page guide called *Funding Education Beyond High School*. (Click on the publications link under "tools and resources" to do so.) The guide walks you through the application process, telling you more than you ever wanted to know about the FAFSA, which stands for Free Application for Federal Student Aid, and the six federal grant and loan programs mentioned above. **You can view this guide in either English or Spanish.**

## Office of Postsecondary Education (OPE)

www.ed.gov/about/offices/list/OPE/index.html

If you want to learn the nitty-gritty details behind student-aid initiatives, stop here for financial-aid news, program highlights, reference materials, and links to OPE's partners in education and government.

## Financial Aid Letters

www.financialaidletter.com

As you wade into the murky waters of financial aid, keep this Web site handy. It will help decipher much of the jargon and confusion. Specifically, this site is perfect for trying to decode exactly what your family will be responsible for financially at your chosen school. Click on sample letters from colleges like the University of California at Davis or the University of Arizona – and then press the "decoder" button to see what the jargon really means. The site is brought to you, free, from the Kiplinger Program in Public Affairs at Ohio State.

## More on Loans

Federal student loans are dispensed under two parallel systems: 1) the Federal Direct Student Loan Program (DSL), in which your loan is made by the federal government directly; and 2) Federal Family Education Loan Program (FFEL) in which your loans come from commercial lenders, such as banks and credit unions. In either case, eligibility, loan limits and interest rates are equivalent, and determined by the federal government. If you apply for federal aid, your college will probably tell you which route to take (some schools participate in direct lending; others do not). In some cases, however, you may be faced with a decision. Which system is better?

This is not an idle question. Legislators, lobbyists, and Department of Education officials have been debating this for the past decade. Private lenders, which make money off the interest subsidies (and gain potential young customers for other banking services), are no fans of direct lending. It cuts them out of the picture. They also say customer service will suffer if the government takes over and the competition among lenders is eliminated. On the other hand, many legislators (mostly Democrats) favor the program, claiming it is more efficient and a better use of taxpayer money.

For now, direct lending and commercial lenders co-exist—with students getting the best end of the deal: better service and better repayment terms, bred by the competition among everybody to prove which system is more efficient. The following sites are most valuable for their information on loans, application deadlines, and repayment plans. But, in the midst of it all, they also offer partisan accounts of both sides of the direct-lending debate.

### The Direct Loan Program
www.ed.gov/DirectLoan

Head for the "Students" page to learn more about Direct Loans, your repayment options, and what happens if you don't pay off your loan. This site is sponsored by the U.S. Department of Education.

### Simple Tuition
www.simpletuition.com

There is nothing better than being able to compare half a dozen loan programs side by side to see which ones offer the best deals. You can do that on this clean and well-organized site. Simple Tuition first helps you make the best choice of federal loans providers, and then—if you need private loans, too—it will allow you to compare those as well. This is a free service; the site makes its money by earning commissions on the loans you eventually pick from its choices offered by 45 different lenders.

### eStudent Loan
www.estudentloan.com

Visit LoanFinder on this site to compare deals on commercial student loans. To get started, you must sign up for a username and password, but after that, the process is quite straightforward. First, you answer a few basic questions, and decide which features are most important to you (for example, lowest APR or lowest overall payment). Then, LoanFinder displays the "best" matches, including links to lender Web sites so you can apply online.

One drawback: LoanFinder only displays a few of the available options (generally four or less), so you can't be certain which loans have been evaluated. Furthermore, some of the biggest lenders do not participate in the service, so if you rely exclusively on LoanFinder you may miss the best deal. This is especially true for students who live in a state that sponsors low-interest loans.

### Sallie Mae
www.salliemae.com

Sallie Mae has provided funds for education loans (primarily federal student loans) for over thirty years, and now either owns or manages over $100 billion in loans for more than ten million borrowers.

The Sallie Mae Web site answers questions about the corporation itself and lets you apply for a variety of loans online. The site also provides online calculators to help you shop for the best repayment plan, and figure out the cost of your loan.

## Banks, Guaranty Agencies, and More

### Yahoo!'s List of Lenders
dir.yahoo.com/Education/Financial_Aid/Loans

An ever-expanding list of lenders, compiled by Yahoo!. You'll find links to banks and other lenders that offer online information about student aid and their educational funding programs. Many of these lenders provide federally-guaranteed loans and give you online access to your loan account. Eventually, you will be able to apply using the FAFSA. For now, you have to contact the lender, and complete a very simple separate application. Most big lenders have now put their loan applications on line.

What follows (in alphabetical order) is a partial list of banks and agencies that provide educational funding, and a wealth of useful college-related information—more financial-aid tips, more information on loan consolidation, more links to student-aid sites, and more calculators to help you determine your best repayment option.

If there is a particular bank you trust for checking or credit-card accounts, you may want to take a look at their student-aid offerings too.

**Access Group**
www.accessgroup.org

**ASAP/Union Bank & Trust**
www.asapubt.com

**Bank of America**
www.bankofamerica.com/studentbanking

**Chase Bank**
www.educationone.com

**Chela Education Financing**
www.chelastudentloans.org

**Citibank**
www.studentloan.com

**College Loan Corporation**
www.collegeloan.com

**Key Education Resources**
www.key.com/education

**LoanStar Education Loans**
www.loanstar.com

**National City**
www.nationalcity.com

**PNC Bank**
www.eduloans.pncbank.com

**Southwest Student Services Corporation**
www.sssc.com

**Student Loan Funding**
www.studentloanfunding.org

**SunTrust Bank**
www.suntrusteducation.com

**US Bank**
www.usbank.com/studentloans

**Wachovia**
www.wachovia.com/personal

**Wells Fargo**
wellsfargo.com/per/accounts/student

## Loan Locator

www.nslc.org

Most banks sell their loans, which means you may get your loan from one institution, but repay it to another. Of course, you are supposed to be notified of this switcheroo; however, if you lose track of your lender, try this nifty service under the "student" section of The National Student Loan Clearinghouse. To use this service, you might need to get additional information from your school's financial aid office.

## State Guaranty Agencies

wdcrobcolp01.ed.gov/Programs/EROD/org_list.cfm

Look down the list of organizations in this Education Resource Directory and click on "State Guaranty Agency." If by some chance you cannot find a lender, contact your state agency. It will either make the loan or point you in the right direction.

As you shop for student loans, look carefully at repayment options—you'll find real differences. For example, some lenders will refund your 3% origination fee. Others reward you for making on-time payments. Common bonuses: forgiving your last six payments or knocking 2% off your interest rate.

# Tax Cuts Explained

(Or, How Do I Get HOPE?)

In August, 1997, Congress passed a tax-relief act that was chock full of educational tax credits and deductions, plus more flexible rules concerning Individual Retirement Accounts (IRAs). The most publicized part of this bill was the HOPE Scholarship program, in which certain taxpayers receive a $1,650 tuition credit for the first two years of post-secondary school. Many parents are now seeing the benefits—if they can figure it all out.

Since then, Congress has approved several additional rounds of tax cuts which expand existing incentives and introduce a few new treats, like a deduction for interest expenses on education loans. The following Web pages should help you keep it all straight.

## IRS's Tax Information for Students

www.irs.gov/individuals/students/index.html

This section offers more than just information about the HOPE scholarship. But it's a good place to start with questions of all kinds related to taxes and students. To drill down to information about HOPE and Lifetime Learning Credits, go to the page devoted to Education Credits (try this whopper of a link to get there directly: www.irs.gov/individuals/article/0,,id=121452,00.html).

IRS Tax Tip 2007-48 explains that The Hope Credit and the Lifetime Learning Credit are education credits you may be able to subtract in full from your federal income tax, not just deduct from your taxable income.

Another method for tax savings is to create a Coverdell Education Savings Account. Here's another unwieldy link to tell you more: www.irs.gov/newsroom/article/0,,id=107636,00.html

In reviewing IRS web sites, remember, they are valuable for their factual information, but not necessarily for their consumer insights.

## Tax Benefits for Education

www.irs.gov/pub/irs-pdf/p970.pdf

This 82-page guide covers the Hope Credit, Lifetime Learning Credit, student loan interest deduction, student loan cancellation, education savings accounts, qualified tuition programs, education savings bonds, employer-provided educational assistance, and business deductions for work-related education expenses.

## The Motley Fool

www.fool.com/taxes/taxcenter

The Motley Fool's TaxCenter includes many articles which will help you understand the impact of the Taxpayer Relief Act of 1997, the Tax Relief Extension Act of 1999, the Economic Growth and Tax Relief Reconciliation Act of 2001, the Jobs and Growth Tax Reconciliation Act of 2003, and assorted other tax relief and reconciliation acts that have passed through Congress over the past four years.

## Kiplinger Tax Center

www.kiplinger.com/taxcenter

A variety of articles to help you make smart tax decision, for example, learn which college savings account to tap first.

# CHAPTER 12

■■■■■■■■■■■■■■■■■■■■■■

## BEYOND UNCLE SAM

After you've figured out how federal grant, loan and tax relief programs work, take a look at what your state offers, what your prospective college might make available, and what private loan programs are out there.

## State Aid

Among states, the numbers and types of scholarship and loan programs vary widely—and new programs such as prepaid tuition plans are popping up everywhere. In most cases, you must be an in-state resident planning to attend an in-state public college to be eligible for this assistance.

### State Education Agencies, State Grant Agencies, and State Higher-Education Agencies
wdcrobcolp01.ed.gov/Programs/EROD/org_list.cfm

Scroll through the directory and look for these three resource lists. "State Education Agencies" links you to each state's main education office; "State Grant Agencies" takes you to information on state-based grants, loans and scholarships; and "State Higher Education Agencies" directs you to each state's higher education commission. Go to the main education department pages for information about the state's policies on everything from K-12 to higher education. Go to the higher education commission for information on specific loan and scholarship packages, as well as other assistance programs for college-bound students.

### College Savings Plans Network
www.collegesavings.org

To encourage early planning for college, every state now sponsors at least one type of college savings programs:

(1) Prepaid Tuition Plans allow parents to guarantee four years of tuition at any of the state's public (or in some cases private) schools by making a lump sum investment of periodic payments.

(2) Savings Plan Trusts give families tax incentives to save for college.

No two programs are the same, and many are not restricted to state residents, so shop around. This site, sponsored by the National Association of State Treasurers, will link you to individual state plans and update you on all the newly-enacted tax incentives (in short, earnings from these plans are now exempt from federal income tax).

### The Internet Guide to 529 Plans
www.savingforcollege.com

Qualified tuition programs (which consist primarily of state-based college savings plans and prepaid tuition plans) are also known as "529 Plans," named for the section of the tax code which clarifies their tax-favored status. Founded by Joseph Hurley, a CPA from New York, this site offers state-by-state comparisons and ratings to help you figure out which plan is best for your family's situation. Plans are evaluated based on their flexibility, liquidity, investment approach, and extra (state) benefits. This last item is especially important—most plans are open to residents of every state, however, they reserve their best terms for locals.

## Collegiate Aid

Be sure to visit the financial-aid Web pages of colleges you are considering. These provide three essentials in your financial-aid quest:

- Information on scholarship and loan programs specific to that college
- Notices of critical deadlines
- News on tuition rates and payment plans.

Here are some easy ways to find them:

### Financial Aid Office Web Pages
www.finaid.org/otheraid/fao.phtml

The FinAid site comes through again. You'll find a fairly comprehensive directory of financial-aid offices—including web sites, e-mail addresses, postal addresses, and phone numbers.

### College and University Aid Offices
www.yahoo.com/Education/Financial_Aid

Yahoo!'s list. Easy to find, but not terribly comprehensive.

If you do not see the college you want listed on the pages above, go to the college's home page. If the home page does not mention financial aid, try sections labeled "admissions," "for entering students" or "student information."

## Focusing on Scholarships

You will find links to these sites on most pages that describe financial aid. The sites have earned reputations for being helpful and free. And because they are helpful and free, there is little reason for you to pay money for some other scholarship search—so don't get suckered by Web sites that ask you to do just that.

### FastWeb

www.fastWeb.com

Financial Aid Search Through the Web. Set aside some time to go through this site, which provides information on nearly 1.3 million scholarship opportunities worth over $3 billion. You have to register and the process takes some time, but the site's producers are honest about telling you that some of the information you supply is given to colleges and "marketing partners." Then fill out the registration pages, being careful not to sign up for any music clubs or magazine subscriptions. . . unless you want to.

You will then wait for a few minutes, while the site pulls its customized information together. The results are worth the wait. You'll find information on scholarships, fellowships, internships, and loans. You can go back to the site every few weeks to see if there are any new opportunities that fit your profile.

You will also receive e-mail messages alerting you to new scholarships that match your search criteria. Each of the entries gives you an overview of the award and several options, including:

1. A link to the sponsor's Web site where you can get more information and (usually) apply online;
2. The ability to print the details, in case you're keeping a paper-based file of scholarship application.

## MACH25

www.collegenet.com/mach25

This site boasts of 600,000 scholarships worth $1.6 billion, however, you don't need to fill out a lengthy questionnaire or divulge any personal information to access them. Instead, you can browse through all the awards, or view them by keyword, for example, "yearbook" or "journalism" or "sports"and decide for yourself which ones are relevant.

## Scholarship Search

www.collegeboard.com/student/pay

This scholarship database contains annually-updated information on scholarships and fellowships from more than 2,300 sources totalling nearly $3 billion. You don't need to register any personal contact information; just answer questions about your affiliations and interests, and your results appear almost immediately. In a test search, the matches were highly relevant to the entered criteria.

Sometimes when you click on a link, an entirely new browser window will open up on your computer screen. Many new sites include this feature, which lets you to click around on one page, without losing track of the index page on which you started. You may find yourself with several open windows, however. Close them when you have finished browsing to keep yourself organized.

## CollegeAnswer (from Sallie Mae)

www.collegeanswer.com

You'll find a free scholarship search under the "paying" tab. It takes about 10-15 minutes to complete a profile form, but once you click the submit button, you can view your results almost immediately. The site says it searches through 2.8 million awards worth $16 billion.

Sallie Mae promises that it will not sell or rent your contact information to third-party vendors, like unwanted advertisers.

## Pacific Northwest Scholarship Guide

www.collegeplan.org/cpnow/pnwguide/pnwguide.htm

If you live in the Pacific Northwest, don't miss this site. The searchable scholarship guide gives you information on hundreds of scholarships available to students who go to school in the Northwest or have parents who work at companies based there.

## The Scholarship Research Network

www.srnexpress.com

This Maryland-based company offers a free (express) service which is worth trying. You'll have to complete a profile, and give out your phone number, but if you do, you'll get to search a fairly comprehensive scholarship database including facts about eligibility, deadlines, and application information.

## The United Negro College Fund

www.uncf.org

The UNCF offers a clearinghouse of thousands of scholarships that can be redeemed at its member colleges, most of which are located in the Southeast (from Virginia to Texas) and are historically-black institutions. You can download the scholarship application straight from the site, but to qualify you must have at least a 2.5 GPA.

The UNCF also administers the $1 billion Gates Millennium Scholarship Program (www.gmsp.org) for low-income minority students and provides details on more than 1000 other scholarships that primarily serve African-American students.

## Black Excel Scholarship Gateway

www.blackexcel.org/link4.htm

Click on the scholarship gateway for information about the above programs, plus more than a dozen other links to scholarships for Native American and African-American students.

## American Society of Association Executives

www.asaenet.org

Many organizations provide scholarships to future members. Under "People and Groups" choose "Directories," then go to "Gateway to Associations" for Web-links to over 11,000 associations. Search for career fields that interest you, click to that association's home page, and learn more about its annual conference, student chapters, and scholarship programs.

### The Foundation Center

www.fdncenter.org/funders

You won't find a scholarship search, just links to more than 80,000 private foundations and corporate grant-makers that may award funds for projects in your area of interest.

## Don't Get Scammed

The Internet is riddled with offers that are a complete waste of money. Fortunately, it also provides sites that warn you about them.

### Scholarship Scams

www.ftc.gov/bcp/conline/edcams/scholarship

Set up by the Federal Trade Commission, this page offers some tips on spotting scholarship scams.

### Evaluating Scholarship Matching Services

www.finaid.org/scholarships/matching.phtml

Another valuable service from FinAid. Helps you evaluate scholarship services and provides advice on protecting yourself from scams.

> Don't mistake a strange suffix like .phtml or .shtml— or even .asp?—for a typo. As the Web becomes more advanced, so does the code behind it. These suffixes are signals telling the Web site to load pages a particular way.

## Considering the Military...

The U.S. Military will generously help you pay for college—if you agree to serve in some capacity for a few or more years. All branches offer ROTC scholarships and let you build (sizable) college funds via the Montgomery GI Bill. Currently, you may receive over $38,000 in education benefits for a three- or four-year enlistment.

The Army sweetens the pot further with its Army College Fund if you enlist in certain "Military Occupation Specialties." (The Navy and Marine Corps have similar benefits.) The Army will also repay up to $65,000 of your federal student loans.

## Military.Com
education.military.com/education-home

An extensive career and education resource center from "Military Advantage," a privately-funded company targeting the military community. You'll get information on the GI Bill, ROTC, and scholarships for servicemembers and dependents.

## ROTC Headquarters
www.defenselink.mil/faq/pis/19.html

Addresses, phone numbers and Web links for each branch of the service.

## The GI Bill
www.gibill.va.gov

Everything there is to know about the GI Bill, courtesy of Uncle Sam.

## My Future
www.myfuture.com

The U.S. Armed Forces have collaborated on a Web site. Here, you'll get an overview of educational (and career) benefits and links to each service.

# ...or Community Service

Volunteering now brings more than just emotional fulfillment. Do good work and you can earn money for college or forgiveness for some of your student loans.

## AmeriCorps, and the Corporation for National Service
www.americorps.org
www.nationalservice.org

AmeriCorps participants receive a modest living allowance, health insurance, and a $4,725 credit per year of full-time service (for a maximum of two years). They may use the credit at any college or graduate school, or to pay off their outstanding student loans. Each year, more than 70,000 students serve in over 3,000 locally-run programs across the United States and their work includes mentoring, disaster relief, and helping to close the digital divide. At the corporation's site, you can look through the AmeriCorps Program Directory to find a project that interests you. You can link to dozens of other worthy organizations that could use your time (but probably won't be able to offer you financial rewards). And, you can browse through a list of colleges that match AmeriCorps awards.

### Presidential Freedom Scholarships

www.learnandserve.gov/about/programs/pfs.asp

Learn how to get nominated for a Presidential Freedom Scholarship. Each high school in the country may select up to two students (juniors and seniors only) to receive these $1,000 awards.

### City Year

www.cityyear.org

With programs in over fifteen American cities plus South Africa, City Year is becoming a nationwide organization of people working to improve their communities. Participants work full-time, five days a week, painting, cleaning, teaching, planting, and tutoring. They receive a small stipend, health insurance, and an end-of-the-year education bonus worth $4,725.

## Aid for Would-be Health Professionals

### National Health Service Corps

nhsc.bhpr.hrsa.gov

### Bureau of Health Professions

www.hrsa.gov/help/healthprofessions.htm

If you are thinking about becoming a doctor or a nurse, you should consider the federal government's programs for health professionals. For example, if you pledge to work in an underserved area, you can get major help in paying for your education from the National Health Service Corps in the form of scholarships and loan repayment.

## If You're an Athlete...

Financial aid takes on a whole new meaning if you are an athlete with talent. But before you drool over possible offers, check the following sites to stay on top of the regulations governing athletic scholarships.

### Guide for the College-Bound Student-Athlete

www.ncaa.org

Under "Academics and Athletes" click on "Eligibility and Recruiting" and you'll find a link to the National Collegiate Athletic Association's *Guide for the College-Bound Student-Athlete*. This guide should be read by every high-school athlete who is serious about getting an athletic scholarship. You will find everything from academic-eligibility requirements to information on agents. The rules about the types of gifts athletes and their families can and cannot accept are very strict. This site is critical to helping you stay within the boundaries.

## NCAA Initial-Eligibility Clearinghouse
www.ncaaclearinghouse.net

To compete at the Division I or II level, you must have your academic eligibility certified by the NCAA clearinghouse. This official site will help you submit your high school courses, grades and SAT/ACT scores for approval. It also provides lists of required high school courses and guides to academic standards.

## National Junior College Athletic Association (NJCAA)
www.njcaa.org

If you are thinking about playing sports at a junior college, don't miss this site. It gives information on athletic scholarships and academic-eligibility requirements. It also offers the full text of its publications. (You will need Adobe Acrobat Reader to view the files, however. Most recent computers come with the software, but for information on downloading it, see the instructions on the NJCAA site.)

With three divisions, and over 500 member schools, the NJCAA represents virtually every community college in the country, but you might want to browse the site's directory anyway—just to make sure the school you want is part of the program.

## Campus Champs
www.campuschamps.com

A helpful and free site with articles and advice about "following your sport into college." Check out the College Spotlight section, which includes summaries of athletic and academic opportunities at dozens of universities.

## Women's Sports Foundation
www.womenssportsfoundation.org

A wonderful resource for female athletes, as well as those interested in a sports career. You'll find fitness information, current news, and a wealth of grants and scholarships.

## Recruitment Services

If you want to spend money (anywhere from $99 - $595) you can hook up with one of these online "recruitment assistance" services. In exchange for your fee, they let you post an athletic profile (and sometimes a 'high-lights' video) where it's available to hundreds (or thousands) of college coaches. For an additional fee, some offer personalized service, as well. Of course, there are no guarantees. And many college coaches still prefer to identify new talent in person (at summer sports camps and high school competitions), or rely on referrals from high school coaches. Here are some of your online options, listed from least costly to most expensive:

### Athletes Advisor
www.athletesadvisor.com

### Scout USA
www.scoutusa.com

### PrepStar
prepstar.com

### College Prospects of America
www.cpoa.com

### College Bound Student Athletes
www.cbsa.com

### National Directory of College Athletics
www.collegiatedirectories.com

If you opt for self-promotion, rather than a fee-based service, visit this site for e-mail addresses of college coaches in your sport. Then send a polite note and description of your athletic accomplishments, and maybe a link to your own Web site so coaches can learn more, and see you in action.

## Commercial Education Loans

If you still need money to help pay the college bills, you might consider a commercial education loan. You can check the following resources or revisit the lenders listed in Chapter 11 (most of them offer their own education loans to supplement their federal student loan offerings). By disclosing your name, address, phone number, social security number, date of birth, income and monthly rent (or mortgage payment), you can usually apply online and learn whether or not you are approved within minutes.

Parents pay attention. If you need help paying college bills, there are dozens of commercial education loans from which to choose so you need to do your homework. Use online calculators and compare interest rates (and interest capitalization policy), loan limits, fees, and repayment options. If you're a home-owner, don't forget to compare the options to a home-equity loan. Quite often, you'll find that's your best deal.

## eStudent Loan
www.estudentloan.com

This site (previously mentioned in Chapter 11) lets you compare a half dozen loan programs side-by-side to see which ones offer the best deals. But remember, some of the biggest lenders do not participate in the service, so if you rely exclusively on LoanFinder you may miss the best deal.

## The Education Resources Institute
www.teri.org

TERI, as it is commonly known, offers loans based on creditworthiness, not income. It provides loans for part-time students, parents, U.S. students in international programs, and more.

## Nellie Mae
www.nelliemae.com

The New England Loan Marketing Association (Nellie Mae) is known for private loans; one is EXCEL, which is designed for parents. But it also offers federally guaranteed loans, such as the PLUS Loan for parents of undergraduates and the Stafford Loan.

## Next Student
www.nextstudent.com

NextStudent features a scholarship search engine as well as access to federal and private student loans, financial advice and a student-loan blog, chock-full of the latest news affecting college loans.

## GATE, or Guaranteed Access to Education
www.gateloan.com

Two loan programs to help with tuition financing: (1) Gate Student Loan Program (through Bank of America) that may be used at over 1500 schools nationwide. (2) College-customized GATE loans that are used by over

75 colleges to supplement financial-aid packages for accepted students. A list of institutions that use GATE is available on this site.

### International Education Finance Corporation
www.IEFC.com

The IEFC offers loans to international students studying in the United States AND to U.S. students studying abroad.

## Installment Plans

Some schools offer interest-free monthly payment plans that let you spread out your tuition payments. Instead of writing two big checks, one at the start of each semester, you write 10 or 12 smaller ones—a considerable boon to your cash flow. These plans are usually administered by an outside agency. For example:

### TuitionPay
www.tuitionpay.com

### Tuition Management Systems
www.afford.com

## A Few More Radical Options ...

### UPromise
www.upromise.com

Shop online at JCrew or Old Navy, Speigel or The Sports Authority, and earn money for college. UPromise has signed up hundreds of partners, including restaurants, credit card companies, and online merchants. Spend money with any of them, and the sponsoring company will put a percentage of your purchase (generally from 2-10%), into a "Section 529" College Savings Plan.

### Sage Tuition Rewards Program
www.sagescholars.com

Parents (or grandparents) who invest with one of Sage's financial partners will earn an undergraduate tuition reduction (at participating colleges) equal to 5% of their average annual account balance up to one full year's tuition. The maximum reward will vary depending on the school you select; currently tuition at participating colleges ranges from $10,800 to $24,700. Example: A $20,000 balance held for five years would earn a tuition reduction reward of $5,000.

If your child decides not to go to one of the nearly 200 participating colleges, the money you've invested is still yours to use as you choose, and the reward amount may be transferred to another student.

## My Rich Uncle

www.myrichuncle.com

MyRichUncle will loan you the funds you need to pay for college. In a twist, your interest rate and repayment terms will be based on your achievements, grades, career plans and goals rather than your present credit history.

## BabyMint

www.babymint.com

BabyMint offers you another way to save for college by shopping, and earning rebates on your purchases. You can then transfer your "BabyMint Bucks" into any "529 Plan." In addition, each dollar you "earn" is matched by a dollar off tuition at nearly 150 "Tuition Rewards"colleges.

## FutureTrust

www.futuretrust.com

Save for college by using your FutureTrust MasterCard. You'll earn a one-percent rebate on all your purchases and up to ten percent by shopping with FutureTrust partners. The rebate goes into a 529 Plan, and if your student attends a "Tuition Rewards" college, all of your rebates will be doubled.

## College Rewards MasterCard

www.fidelity.com

This card puts 2% of everything you spend into a Fidelity-managed 529 Plan to a maximum of $1,500 per year.

## College Tuition Match

www.collegetuitionmatch.com

This site is still more of a concept than a working service. But the mission is to become something like a Priceline.com for colleges and students where colleges accept students' bids for tuition. The site lets students register for free then sends their profiles to colleges and universities. The participating schools take a look at the profiles and if they like any of them, they pay CTM a $100 fee to learn the identity of the student, so they can work out the admission and financial aid details.

# PART FIVE

■ ■ ■ ■ ■ ■ ■ ■ ■ ■ ■ ■ ■ ■ ■ ■ ■ ■

## IF YOU'VE PROCRASTINATED
## FOR TOO LONG . . .

## Annual Student Vacancy Survey

www.nebhe.org/vacancy_survey.html

If you'd like to go to college in the New England area, but wonder if it's too late, visit this site (between May and August) to look through the annual vacancy survey. You may be surprised at how many colleges are still taking applications (and still offer financial aid). Browse for openings at over 200 colleges in Connecticut, Maine, Massachusetts, New Hampshire, Rhode Island, and Vermont.

## NACAC Space Availability Survey

www.nacacnet.org/MemberPortal

Each spring, the National Association of College Admission Counselors (NACAC) surveys its members and compiles a list of colleges and universities that have not yet met their fall enrollment goals. And each spring, NACAC posts the results (but don't look for it during the fall and winter). The NACAC survey also gives information on available housing and unclaimed financial aid.

If you have trouble accessing the site, you may also request a copy of the results by calling NACAC's fax-on-demand, (703) 299-6829.

# PART SIX

## Cyber-College Life

# CHAPTER 13

■■■■■■■■■■■■■■■■■■■■■

## THE FUN STUFF

You've finished! The search process is over, the SAT is history, the admission applications are sitting in some dean's office waiting to be reviewed, and the financial-aid applications are in the mail. It's time to sit back, relax, and dream of what college will be like.

Or maybe you are just taking a break. Either way, here are a few fun spots, listed alphabetically, to give you a glimpse of cyber-college life.

## #1 Free Stuff
www.1freestuff.com

Start practicing for your starving-student days by checking out all the fun things you can get for free!

## The Black Collegian Online
www.black-collegian.com

Get a monthly dose of information about post-college career opportunities. Here you'll also find commentary by leading African-American writers, entertainment features, and general information on college life.

## Campus Access
www.campusaccess.com

Although it was designed for Canadian college students, this site is brimming with information that can help any first-year student, anywhere. Read essays about how to get prepared for independence, how to choose a major, how to take notes, and how to survive if you can't stand your roommates.

## Campus Circle
www.campuscircle.net

Online source for college entertainment. Special sections for music, film, news, DVDs and lifestyle.

## CampusEstore.com

www.campusestore.com

Get discounts on computer equipment, software, electronics and more. These discounts are only available to college students. But if you are a high-school senior who has been accepted to college, you too can participate. To get in, you must send a copy of your acceptance letter.

 If you're using a slow machine, beware. Most of these sites are graphics-heavy. And if you turn off the images function on your browser, some of what makes these fun will disappear.

## College Club

www.collegeclub.com

The folks at College Club have pumped up their site—adding e-mail and instant message services, 24-hour chat rooms, interactive polls, online forums, discount directories, personal home pages, Web cams, you name it. College students (and college-bound students, too) may register for free.

## Collegiate Standard Online

www.collegiatestandard.com

The official publication of the North Carolina Collegiate Association, which says it publishes the best of writing, art and photography from North Carolina college students. Don't miss the article, "Effortless Perfection, " a true and troubling account of the pressures of fitting in at Duke University. The writer could have been at any number of top colleges, and she has done many students a service by bringing attention to the problems of too many high expectations.

## DORM Store

www.dormtours.net/eshop.asp

Take a virtual tour of actual college dorm rooms, so you know what to expect, then go e-shopping to recreate the coolest looks. This site also lets you "register" for stuff, in case your friends and relatives want to give you a going-away-to-college present.

## GreekChat

www.greekchat.com

This site is dedicated to message boards and chat. It works best with up-to-date browsers—the sites use the latest java technology.

## GreekPages

www.greekpages.com

Here's the place to get a sense of what fraternity and sorority members around the country are talking about. The site, which is updated regularly, also provides links to "hellenistic" chapters with innovative Web sites.

## The Internet Guide to Spring Break

www.springbreak.com

Dreaming of a sun-baked week with your new college buddies? Check out this site during the spring break season (March and April) to see live beach Web cams of hot spots. Until then, find out about last year's "kewl" destinations, and take a peek at yearbooks of previous spring breaks.

## mtvU

www.mtvu.com

Owned by MTV, mtvU plays a mix of music ranging from hip hop to rock. It also also sponsors a variety of contests and features segments on everyday campus life—food, fashion, sports, travel, and more.

## Pick-a-Prof

www.pick-a-prof.com

Start studying up on your future professors. Pick-a-Prof is still expanding, but if your school is included, you can get an advance peek at a professor's lecture style, attendance policy, grading history, and more. The reviews are written by students; the grade distributions are compiled directly from university records (thanks to state open record laws).

## Roommate Service.Com

www.roommates.com

If you plan to live off-campus, this site, with over 150,000 listings, can help you find the perfect roommate.

## StudentAdvantage.Com

www.studentadvantage.com

Works with thousands of merchants to develop (and sell) products for students in categories ranging from dorm decor to wireless and telecom.

## The Student Center

www.student.com

The Student Center serves up sassy articles on campus culture, jobs and travel. Also relationship advice, personal ads, and links to hundreds of student diaries. You can even go to the "casino" and play a quick game of Texas Hold 'Em (for points, not cash).

## Student Counselng Virtual Pamphlet Collection

www.dr-bob.org/vpc

This site links to hundreds of virtual pamphlets published by an assortment of university counseling centers. Topics include alcohol and substance abuse, sexual harassment, study skills, test-taking and time management.

## U Magazine from Colleges.com

www.colleges.com/Umagazine/index.html

Read through current and past issues of U.Magazine, a tabloid that is distributed on campuses.

## The Universal Black Pages

www.ubp.com

Link into a bunch of educational information, including home pages of historically black colleges, African-American student groups, fraternities, and sororities. The site contains links to non-college resources too.

## For more e-zines, try the lists at Yahoo! or Google

dir.yahoo.com/News_and_Media/College_and_University/Magazines

www.google.com/Top/News/Colleges_and_Universities/
Magazines_and_E-zines

# CHAPTER 14

■ ■ ■ ■ ■ ■ ■ ■ ■ ■ ■ ■ ■ ■ ■ ■ ■ ■ ■ ■ ■

## E-CAMPUS BOOKSTORES
## AND ONLINE LECTURE NOTES

## On line or In line?

Online book buying is becoming a popular replacement for waiting in line with arms aching from baskets of heavy books.

Most freshmen wait until they arrive on campus before buying their textbooks—and experiencing sticker shock. But the Web can give you a head start. If you already know your classes, head to Amazon or Barnes & Noble online, or a textbook-oriented e-bookseller with your credit card (or, more likely, your parents' credit card) ready. You can save up to 40 percent on the cost of new books, and, sometimes, have them delivered for free. Many bookselling sites offer other college-related merchandise too—so check their prices before you head out for a back-to-school spree.

If you want to play it safe and wait until school starts, you should still take a look at these e-booksellers and familiarize yourself with how they work—in addition to discounts on new books, they usually offer a large selection of used textbooks, as well as book buybacks and discounts for referring your book-buying friends. And, if you're still trying to decide between courses, peeking at reading lists can help you make your decision.

### Best Book Buys
www.bestbookbuys.com

To use this nifty site, simply enter a book's title, author, keyword or ISBN. BestBookBuys then searches through 27 different online bookstores and displays the price, availability, shipping method and shipping charges at each. For example, total costs for a new copy of Marilyn Stokstad's *Art History* (3rd ed.) ranged from $94 to $136; a used copy was only $79.

## EFollett

www.Efollet.com

Follett has been a family-owned business for over 125 years and manages hundreds of college bookstores across the country. EFollet joins over 900 of those bookstores in an e-partnership. Follet's Internet site organizes book lists by college, and offers both new and used texts. Follet will ship books to you (for a fee), or, you can arrange to pick up your order on-campus.

## VarsityBooks.com

www.varsitybooks.com

New and used textbooks. You can search by title, author or ISBN.

## Big Words

www.bigwords.com

Like BestBookBuys, this site searches online stores and returns a list of book options for you to pursue. It also features a book buy-back option.

## E Campus

www.ecampus.com

Another e-bookstore; this one has a lucrative buy-back program. Just enter your book's ISBN and learn the buy-back price; sometimes you'll get as much as 50% of the purchase price. ECampus also offers online auctions and special deals on computers, clothes and DVDs.

## ClassBook.com

www.classbook.com

Another site to buy and sell new and used textbooks.

Publishers assign every edition of every book a unique ten-digit ISBN ("International Standard Book Number"). You'll find this identifying number on the book's back cover (as part of the bar code), or on an inside page, with the copyright information.

# Class Notes On the Web

Don't want to go to class? No problem. Sleep in, then download the day's lecture notes from the comfort of your dorm room. That is the pitch of a new breed of sites which provide class notes, free of charge, via the Web.

Lecture note sites employ students from across the country to post class notes to their specific area of the site. The 'guides' or 'tutors' maintain their area with up-to-date reports on class meetings, topic-driven chats, and even host study sessions before exams.

Do commercial sites have the right to publish class notes? Legal issues over intellectual property are now playing out in the courts, and the main "class notes" sites from previous editions of *College.edu* have disappeared into thin cyber-air. Some universities, like MIT and Utah State, however, have simply decided to beat these companies at their own game, and distribute their own course lecture notes (freely) on the Web.

### MIT's OpenCourseWare
ocw.mit.edu

The Massachusetts Institute of Technology has committed $100 million to OpenCourseWare, and will go online with lecture notes, course outlines, reading lists and homework assignments for all 2,000 of its courses over the next few years (1,550 courses are already available). This site is completely free of charge, so anyone in the world can benefit from an MIT education, minus the classroom interaction between faculty and student (which MIT notes is the "fundamental cornerstone" of its learning process).

Course materials are in the process of being translated into several additional languages, starting with Spanish, Portugese and Chinese.

Following MIT's lead, many other schools are in the process of putting course materials on the Web. The list of members can by found at ocwconsortium.org. Here are a few examples:

### Utah State's OpenCourseWare
ocw.usu.edu

### Notre Dame
ocw.nd.edu

### Tufts' OpenCourseWare
ocw.tufts.edu

### Johns Hopkins School of Public Health
ocw.jhsph.edu

## Open Courseware Consortium
ocwconsortium.org

As new members come online, you'll find them listed here.

# Cheater-Catchers

While the Web has made it easier to access contraband educational material, it has also added new weapons to the arsenals of teachers trying to curb plagiarism. Several sites let teachers match text strings that 'seem suspicious' to documents that are available online. They simply enter a sentence or two from a student's paper and find out if the exact or similar phrase appears somewhere on the Web. It is then up to the professor to visit the site and judge whether the passage in question is indeed plagiarized, or simply cut from a similar idea.

The mere existence of these paper-matching sites is enough to keep most students from purchasing papers online.

## TurnItIn.com
www.turnitin.com

Chief among these sites is Turn It In which compares provided text with millions of web pages and the archives of dozens of free term paper sites. Its "Originality Reports" include an "overall similarity index" and color-coded links to contested passages.

## Plagiarism.org
www.plagiarism.org

This central resource provides a clear explanation of the technologies used to detect digital plagiarism.

## Essay Verification Engine (EVE)
www.canexus.com/eve

This low-cost download ($29.99/user) accepts essays in plain text, Microsoft Word, or Corel Word Perfect and returns links to web pages from which a student may have plagiarized. If it finds evidence of plagiarism, the URL is recorded. Once the search has completed, the teacher is given a full report on each paper that contained plagiarism, including the percent of the essay plagiarized, and an annotated copy of the paper showing all plagiarism highlighted in red. (And "yes," we "plagiarized" this description from the company's Web site.)

# APPENDIX 1

■■■■■■■■■■■■■■■■■■■■

## METASITES

These sites attempt to be all things to all people. They have advice for parents and students, tips on choosing and applying, resources on financial aid, college essays, you name it. I call them metasites, and depending on your personality or the information you are looking for, they just might become your favorite stop on the Internet. They are arranged in alphabetical order, so their placement does not reflect quality. If a site seems to have gaps or disadvantages, you'll see that noted.

### About.Com's College Admissions page
collegeapps.about.com

A section devoted to information for college-bound students and their parents. Read about everything from scholarship myths and misconceptions to distance-learning programs.

> Most of these sites require you to "sign in" or "register" before you can peek inside (or at least get to the good stuff). By disclosing this information, you are helping the site show its advertisers that people of your demographic profile are clicking around. You're also giving it useful information for marketers and advertisers. Neither of which is necessarily bad—but you should know how these sites work.

### America Online's College Prep area

In AOL, go to keyword "college," and you'll find a bunch of stuff on financial aid, links to articles and Web sites that help narrow your search, plus useful links for the college bound.

### Black Excel
www.blackexcel.org

Read about historically black colleges, learn about the black greek experience, and browse through the directory of black student unions at colleges across the country. The site also offers admissions advice and a gateway to scholarship services.

### Careers and Colleges

www.careersandcolleges.com

A colorful site stocked with tools for anyone, including a college search, scholarship search and loan search, as well as admission and financial aid advice and career information.

### College Answer

www.collegeanswer.com

Sponsored by student-loan behemoth Sallie Mae, College Answer has folders on preparing, selecting, applying and paying for college, as well as interactive tools to help you evaluate your financial-aid award letters and make your final college decision.

### College Board Online

www.collegeboard.com

Take some time to dig through all the material. You'll find a guide to campus visits, columns about what admission officers look for in applicants, financial-aid calculators, and online registration for the SAT. There is also a section for education professionals, including high-school counselors.

### College Confidential

www.collegeconfidential.com

With a heavy emphasis on Ivy League admissions, this site offers a college search engine, admission tips and a campus survival guide.

### CollegeNET

www.collegenet.com

Includes MACH25, the scholarship search described in Chapter 12. Also offers electronic applications for hundreds of schools, a database of college information, links to financial-aid hot spots, and some virtual tours.

### College Planning

www.collegeplan.org

A fantastic resource for students living in the Pacific Northwest—and a still-valuable site for students living elsewhere. Search the scholarship guide, read the keys to college selection and admission, and take a walk through the "money maze."

## CollegePrep 101

collegeprep.okstate.edu

This site was developed by the College of Education at Oklahoma State University. It includes everything from college terminology to recruitment materials to stress management to what's trendy on campuses today.

## College Solutions Network

www.csnamerica.com

You'll find college admissions help, test prep, a scholarship search, and student loan information.

## CollegeView

www.collegeview.com

The site, published by Hobsons Publishing, offers numerous articles on the college-planning process as well as a database of information searchable by college, with the option to "zap" quick e-mail inquiries to the colleges of your choice.

## FinAid Page

www.finaid.org

A one-stop shop for information about student loans, federal programs, scholarship services, and more. This resource can't be beat. Compiled and updated by Mark Kantrowitz, a Web publisher and financial-aid expert.

## Go College

www.gocollege.com

College and scholarship searches, expert advice, practice tests, distance learning, campus bookstore and campus entertainment.

## Guidance On-Line

home.cfl.rr.com/nwunder/guidance.html

A useful list of links to college search pages, financial-aid sites, scholarship data bases, and more. Updated regularly by Olympia High School in Orlando, Florida.

## My College Guide

www.mycollegeguide.org

This site lets you search for a college, ask questions of the admission guru, download the common application, or read a free issue of *My College Guide* magazine. Updated monthly.

## MyRoad.com

myroad.collegeboard.com/myroad/navigator.jsp

This site, acquired by The College Board, offers something many of the others don't: advice for students who first want to figure out their career paths and then choose a college based on those plans. Free for students in the year they take the PSAT/NMSQT. Others must pay an annual fee of $19.95. If you decide to pay for it, the site also provides a searchable database of colleges as well as information about the job market.

## National Association for College Admission Counseling

www.nacacnet.org/MemberPortal/News/StepsNewsletter

Hundreds of articles on every aspect of the admission and financial aid process.

## Peterson's Education Portal

www.petersons.com

Brought to you by Peterson's, the long-time publisher of college guides. This well-designed site includes news and announcements, test prep, college search services, online applications, financial aid and scholarship data, and—of course—promos for Peterson's books.

## Princeton Review

www.princetonreview.com

In addition to test-prep, this site offers online applications, a scholarship search, and a database of college information. Also provides career advice and tells students what to pack for college. The site's forums are one of its most interesting features, with postings from hundreds of students.

## ScholarStuff

www.scholarstuff.com

This site does not provide much original content, but it does a decent job collecting hundreds of useful links to college-related sites on the Web. It's also a good stop for links to international universities and information on sororities and fraternities.

■ ■ ■ ■ ■ ■ ■ ■ ■ ■ ■ ■ ■ ■ ■ ■

# Thinking Ahead:

# Getting Ready for Graduate School

*College.edu* focuses on college planning for undergraduates; however, there are numerous web sites that will help you get ready for graduate school as well. Meta-sites for Med School, Law School and Business School are especially plentiful, so if you think there's an MCAT, LSAT or GMAT in your future, here's a site sampler to get you started.

## Student Doctor Network

www.studentdoctor.net

This site contains useful information for medical students, dental students and allied health students. You'll find advice on getting in (and getting through) med school, financial aid information, residency listings, and health care career information. You can also read medical student diaries and participate in forums and chat rooms. And, you can navigate through over 1000 links, including e-books, health care humor and sites for pre-med students.

## FindLaw for Law Students

stu.findlaw.com/prelaw

Lots of articles, on lots on useful topics—Considering Law School, Financing Law School, Law School Admission Information, Law School Rankings, Pre-Law Discussion Forums, Pre-Law Organizations and Preparing for Law School.

## Internet Legal Resource Guide

www.ilrg.com/pre-law.html

Brought to you by current students at The University of Texas School of Law, this site will link you up with a variety of pre-law services, like LSAT preparation, pre-law advising programs, first year prep courses, and dozens of law school rankings.

## Law Jobs and Career Center

www.law.com/jsp/law/careercenter/index.jsp

Interesting news articles as well as career information and "Advice for the Lawlorn," a weekly Q&A section hosted by a past president of the National Association of Legal Search Consultants.

## MBA.com

www.mba.com

The Graduate Management Admission Council has developed this search engine to help you choose the right MBA program for you. This site will also help you prepare for the GMAT, link up with financial aid possibilities, and develop effective job search strategies.

# APPENDIX 2

■■■■■■■■■■■■■■■■■■■■■

Feeling left behind? Still unsure what people mean when they talk about bookmarks, browsers, and bad links? The following questions and answers should help you catch up. For those who already understand Internet basics, skip ahead. Some answers at the end—such as how Wi-Fi works—just might teach you something you don't yet know.

## What is the Internet?

The Internet is one enormous INTERNational NETwork of computers that can communicate with each other. Some are connected by MODEMS, which are machines that make connections using telephone lines. (This is the case for most people who use the Internet at home.) Many are linked by high-speed lines and cables, which allow much faster communication. And a few are connected via satellites.

The communication that occurs on this enormous network can take many forms. Electronic mail, or E-MAIL, is one of the simplest forms. In e-mail, a single message is sent from one computer to another. Newsgroups and the World Wide Web are more complex.

## What are newsgroups? Usenet?

Newsgroups are the Internet's community kiosks. USENET (a huge 'user's network') links most of them together. People post hundreds of announcements, questions, and pieces of advice in some 50,000 newsgroups each day. Most material posted in newsgroups is junk—but you never know when something helpful might turn up.

Newsgroups started before the days of the Web, and used to be available only with "newsreader" software. Today, the easiest way to browse through newsgroups is via your Internet browser, or Google at groups.google.com. Google lets you search the entire newsgroup system for one "article" or post, or search for a specific newsgroup topic. (For more on newsgroups, see Chapter 1.)

## What is the World Wide Web?

The Web is a subset of the Internet made up of picture, sound, and text files located on computers around the world that can be viewed by people on other computers around the world. The Web brought the Internet alive by giving it color, images, and easy-to-use commands.

## What is HTML?

For a file to be "viewable" on the Web, it must be coded using HTML, or hypertext markup language. HTML can be read by any Web browser—regardless of whether the computer is a Macintosh, Windows-based PC, or Unix machine.

## What is a URL?

Universal Resource Locator. This is cyberlingo for the path or address of a particular site. URLs on the Web usually look something like this: www.site.com/lookhere.html

## What does http://www.site.com/lookhere.html mean?

"http" signifies the material is available on the Web. "www.site.com" is called the domain name. Think of it as the storage center for the files you're viewing. The rest of the address, in this case "lookhere.html," tells your Web browser exactly which files to display from that storage area.

## What do ".com," ".edu," ".gov" ".org" and ".mil" mean?

These domains denote whether a site is run by a commercial company (.com), an institution of higher education (.edu), a government site (.gov), a non-profit organization (.org) or the military (.mil). Outside the United States, names end in abbreviations for the country, such as .ca for Canada.

The domain '.edu' is usually a reliable indicator—most Web sites with '.edu' suffixes are in fact universities or colleges. But some not-so-kosher companies will assign themselves a '.edu' suffix even though they are not non-profits, are not accredited, and are not institutions of higher learning. Until domain names are better regulated, Net surfers should never assume a Web site is legitimate simply because it uses '.edu' in its address.

## What is a Web browser?

Netscape Navigator and Microsoft Internet Explorer are Web browsers. There are other less common ones as well. Web browsers are instruments for viewing HTML files. All browsers contain a field where a person can enter the path, or URL, for a Web page. Once the path is entered, the browser displays its contents in the window below. Browsers also contain a "status bar" to show you the address of your current URL; scroll bars to help you move up and down pages more quickly; "back" and "forward" buttons to let you move back and forth between sites you've already visited; a "favorite" or "bookmark" icon to help you add and organize your favorite sites; and a "stop" button to interrupt file transfers (very useful when you get tired of waiting for a slow file to load).

## What is a home page?

Generally, a home page is a file that stakes out a person's or organization's place on the Web. A university's home page is the front page of its Web site, which could contain hundreds of interior pages.

## What is hypertext?

When using the Web, you will see words that are highlighted in color and underlined. These are the most common form of hyperlinks. When you click on hyperlinks and arrive at new pages with more hyperlinked words, you are experiencing hypertext. It is a nonlinear way of reading texts and examining images, in which a person can find out what is "behind" the word simply by clicking on it.

## What is the difference between dial-up and broadband access? And why do some sites take so long to load?

The Internet's speed is usually based on four major factors: 1) the speed of the connection from your computer to the outside world, 2) the volume of traffic on the Internet, 3) the amount of material you are trying to transmit, and 4) the speed of the connection on the computer holding the files you are trying to view.

If you are using a computer that connects to the Internet via a broadband connection, you will find that pages load much more quickly. Theoretically, the speed can be hundreds of times faster than with a dial-up modem (see below). Computers with broadband access are most commonly found in places with heavy Internet usage, such as your high school, your parents' office, or your local library. But in the past two years, the number of households with broadband access has soared. These homes usually connect to the Internet via cable or DSL (digital subscriber line). Call your phone or cable company to sign up. Typically the rate is about $40 a month.

If you are using a dial-up MODEM, you will often have to wait for pages to load—especially if the site contains a lot of hefty material, such as photographs, animated pictures, and large text files.

## So what can I do about the slowness?

If you are still using a dial-up connection to get on the Internet, here are a few tricks to help you avoid traffic jams and slow-loading pages:

Most Web browsers give you the option of NOT loading images. This means you will only be able to view text. Where images should be you'll see what are called "BROKEN GRAPHICS," which are the symbols for image files that do not show up properly on your browser. Well-designed Web sites will provide alternative text as replacements for broken graphics so that you may still get a sense of what is being shown on the page.

To take advantage of this option, you'll have to change your "preferences" or preferred settings. In Netscape Navigator, you'll find these settings by pulling down the "edit" menu, choosing "preferences," and then "advanced" settings. From there you can un-check the box labeled "automatically upload images." On Internet Explorer, pull down the "tools" menu, select "Internet options" and go to the "advanced" area. You'll find the box labeled "show pictures" under the heading "multimedia."

Also, advanced browsers allow you to decide whether you want to receive the images during or after the text of the page has loaded. Select the "after" option so that you will be able to read the page while the computer cranks out the graphics.

Finally, you may want to be selective about when you get on line. Avoid Internet rush hours, such as weekday evenings and weekend afternoons. Avoid big news days, like election day, when the Internet will be clogged with too many users as well.

## What does Wi-Fi mean? How can I get access?

Wi-Fi is short for wireless fidelity. It has become the commonplace term for the network that enables people to connect to the Internet without wires or cables, using the radio spectrum instead.

If you have a relatively new laptop, for instance, you probably have a built-in wireless card that can detect whenever you are in range of a Wi-Fi hotspot, where wireless devices are strategically placed to send out signals allowing you to get on the Net. Coffeeshops like Starbucks and public libraries are becoming known for being Wi-Fi hotspots.

Some hotspots are free; you can just open up your Web browser and surf away (though you may first have to log on or click on a link that appears on your screen). Others are subscriber-based services, like T-Mobile, which lets you buy a few hours' worth of access or several months-worth of time using its network.

For maps showing over 24,000 free Wi-Fi hotspots in the United States and more information on how to use them, go to www.openwifispots.com.

## What are bookmarks? How do I save them from one computer to another?

Bookmarks got their name from Netscape; other brands use words like Internet Explorer's "Favorites" or AOL's "Favorite Places." These are handy lists of sites you have seen once and want to visit again.

When you "bookmark" a page, you are saving the address to a file on your hard drive. Your bookmarks, therefore, are not very portable—unless you set your browser to save them on a disk instead. Under the word "bookmarks" on Netscape, click on "go to bookmarks" or "edit book-marks." Under the file menu, you'll see a "save as" option, which will allow you to save the bookmarks to a diskette or a networked drive. Most other browsers give you the same option.

When you go to another computer and want to use these bookmarks, pop in your disk, open "go to bookmarks" or "edit bookmarks" and choose "open" under the file menu. You'll then be able to retrieve them from the A: drive.

To organize your slew of bookmarked sites, use your Web browser to set up folders according to categories you design. For example, you might want one folder for your list of favorite colleges, another for your materials on financial aid, and a third for all the fun stuff in Chapter 13.

## How does e-mail work on the Web?

Most people use e-mail on an online service like America Online or on a local Internet service provider. (The latest versions of Netscape and Internet Explorer provide their own e-mail services, as do many Web sites.) But sometimes a Web page will provide a HYPERTEXT LINK TO AN E-MAIL ADDRESS. When you click on that address, a window will open in which you can type a message and hit send.

If you are on a computer at home, feel free to use this option. If it is your first time using e-mail on Netscape, for example, you will often get a message asking you to set your return e-mail address. To do that, follow the directions given, which differ depending on the browser you are using.

But if you are on someone else's computer—such as the one in your high-school library—avoid using Web-based e-mail. If you see a link to an e-mail address, write the address down and use it later, when you are on your own e-mail system. Sending a message from someone else's computer means the return address is also someone else's. If the person receiving your e-mail hits the "reply" button, he or she will be replying to that e-mail address instead of yours. (Some administrators have "locked" the e-mail mechanism on public computers so this won't happen—but you can never be too sure.)

Here's a tip: Always write your e-mail address after your name when you send e-mail. That way, if the message is ever truncated or forwarded, the recipient will still have an address for you.

Some e-mail programs let you create "signature files" which automatically attach to the end of each e-mail message (or newsgroup posting). You can use this "sig" for all your contact information, like your full name, mailing address, e-mail address, phone number, and high school name. Keep it under five lines, and avoid including "meaningful" quotes, or unnecessary personal data.

In choosing your e-mail name, use your real name (or your first initial and last name). Admission officers won't be impressed by a letter from someone named Bob2Cool or KittyKat.

## How about free e-mail services?

If you do not have your own Web connection, you can sign up for a free e-mail account with BigFoot (www.bigfoot.com), HotMail (hotmail.com), CollegeClub (www.collegeclub.com), Mail.com (www.mail.com), or Lycos (mail.lycos.com), as well as with other large search engines like Yahoo! (mail.yahoo.com) or Google (gmail.google.com). Your messages will be stored on the sponsoring company's server, not your own, so you can easily check your e-mail from any computer with an Internet connection.

There are several other advantages to setting up a free e-mail account (even if you do have your own computer). First, you can use this name when you register with all the college search sites. This should reduce the amount of junk e-mail that finds its way into your "real" account. Second, if you absolutely must have a funky online moniker, you can use free accounts to change your persona every week. Third, if you plan to visit chat rooms, you can use your alternate name. Again, this should help limit the junk e-mail that would otherwise clog up your regular mail box.

On the downside, free e-mail accounts come with lots of advertisements (which is why they are "free"), and they can be quite slow.

### If I don't use one of these free e-mail services, how can I check my e-mail when I'm away from my home?

Assuming you have a computer with Internet access, Mail2Web makes it simple to tap into your ISP and retrieve your e-mail. Just log onto www.mail2web.com, enter your e-mail address (or IP Address) and password, and this utility does the rest. It now supports AOL email as well.

If you are accessing from your PDA, use www.mail2web.com/pda; if you have a WAP (wireless application protocol) compatible mobile phone, dial www.mail2web.com/wap.

### How can I make sure my e-mail is private?

When you send an e-mail message, you are sending the equivalent of a postcard. If that message is ever intercepted, it can be read by anyone who happens to pick it up. So if you are sending something confidential or if you have a touch of paranoia, you may want to check out the latest private e-mail services. A company called ZixMail, for example, offers the equivalent of locked envelopes in which you may transport your messages (www.zixcorp.com). It requires downloadable software and costs money, but it will work with almost any mail system including AOL.

A similar service is offered by HushMail.com.

### What are viruses, and how do I avoid them?

Viruses are nasty, replicable programs that can infect your computer's hard drive. Viruses can be minor nuisances that change the way a particular program runs or they can corrupt your entire operating system.

If you use virus-scanning software like that offered by Symantec or McAfree, you can usually rest assured that you aren't unknowingly bringing viruses into your computer. Most computers at schools and libraries have this type of "disinfectant" to ward off viruses.

If you don't know whether the computer you are using has virus-checking software, you might want to refrain from putting anything unknown onto your hard drive. Viruses can only get to your hard drive if they have access to it—so if you never download anything or insert any unknown diskettes into your computer, you should be fine.

You cannot catch viruses from e-mail messages or Web-surfing, unless you download an infected file. The ILOVEYOU virus that gained popularity was an "attachment" to an E-mail message. It could only be activated by being opened, which is typically done by clicking on the attachment icon that comes in the e-mail message. Never click on an attached file unless you know what it is and why it was sent to you.

To avoid viruses on diskettes, use only those that have been inserted into computers you are familiar with. Nearly all the plug-ins and other downloadable files noted in this book have been secured by Web site owners to ensure that they are safe from viruses.

## Where do America Online and Microsoft Network fit in?

These are nationwide, commercial providers of Internet services. In addition to connecting you to the Internet complete with your own e-mail addresses, they provide their own content—which is available only to those who have signed up with their network.

## What are search engines? Where do I find them?

Search engines are the Web's saving grace. For example if you are looking for a site on college football but you don't have a specific URL, go to a search engine like Yahoo!, Google or others, and type the words "college football." The search engine will point you to related sites.

Search engines aren't perfect however—not by a long shot. Some Web sites never turn up in an Internet search, while others pop up all the time—even though their links haven't worked for months. And some Web sites pop up all the time, even though they aren't what you are looking for, because the site's designer has manipulated the system to rise to the top.

So to get the most out of your search engine, you should know some basics about how they work. First, learn the difference between a **raw search** of the Web, which pulls up links to anything out there, and a search of an **already-compiled directory** of Web sites reviewed by human beings. If you are looking for something obscure, you probably want to search the entire Web. If you want something more common, like "college football," then you will have the most luck with an already-compiled directory.

Fortunately, the most popular search services now allow you to do both. Here are some examples.

## www.google.com

No frills. Very fast. You can search the entire Web, or look through specific categories, images, or pdf files. And you seldom come across bad addresses, since Google takes a snapshot of every page it examines and stores it as a "cached" link. In other words, if the page you're looking for is currently unavailable, you can view it as it last appeared to Google.

FYI: Googol equals the number "1" followed by 100 zeroes.

If you're a frequent Google user, you can save yourself time by installing the Google toolbar—at toolbar.google.com—and using it to do searches without having to always go to the Google homepage.

## www.yahoo.com

Categorizes hundreds of thousands of Web sites—and if those sites don't provide what you want, Yahoo! also searches the entire Web. Yahoo! was one of the first search services on the Web and to this day it is the most popular.

## www.alltheweb.com

This search engine has a refreshing inclination to find non-American pages—a byproduct of its Norwegian roots. In fact, you can search in 36 different languages. It's also got a huge index—provided by Yahoo!—sometimes challenging Google in size.

## www.ask.com

A clean and simple interface (google-style), but with a slightly different formula for pulling up matches to your keywords. (The site uses technology developed by Teoma, which was once a stand-alone search engine.) Offers blog searching and localized searches that come with maps.

## www.altavista.com

More browsable directories plus full-Web searches, multimedia searches, and tools like e-mail, radio and the yellow pages. Also includes Babel Fish Translation, a feature that instantly translates websites (or plain text) from one language into another. Very Quickly.

> As the Web expands, search engines are less and less helpful for non-specific searches. If you type a single common word like "college" or "scholarship," you'll end up with tens of thousands of sites to visit—clearly, a daunting journey.

## AOL Search

AOL's search service allows you to search for information inside AOL and out on the Web—simultaneously. Use the "search" toolbar on the "Welcome" screen, and become adept at clicking among "Recommended Sites" and "Matching Sites." AOL Search is now enhanced by Google.

## www.live.com
Microsoft revamped its search engine, opting for the streamlined look à la Google.

## www.lycos.com
A hub for searching the Web and browsing categories. Includes news, multimedia searching, and parental controls.

# Meta-Search Engines

If you're looking for something really obscure, you may want to use several search engines at one time. Fortunately Meta-search engines make that possible. They run searches on multiple search engines at one time, and bring you the results. Here are the ones I have the most luck with:

## www.dogpile.com
"Fetches" results by more than a dozen different search engines — and includes several other features to boot. You can search news wires and Usenet, yellow pages, white pages, online auctions, and MP3 files. For regional searches, try Dogpile's geographically-tailored search service. And if you simply want a browsable catalog of sites, Dogpile offers that, too.

## www.mamma.com
"The mother of all search engines." This new meta search provides results quickly, and tells you which search engine was used to find the answer.

## www.search.com
Brought to you by CNet, an online source of product reviews and technology news.

## www.metacrawler.com
This metasearch allows you to customize your search screen by specifying whether you want to search specific domains, like the .edu domain, and lets you select the search engines that you would like to use simultaneously.

### How can I get better search results?
Think about what you are searching for. Are you looking for Web sites that relate to commonly understood and broad topics, like shopping or travel? If so, try the human-compiled directories like Yahoo. If you are looking for something very specific, like a rare surname, try a pure search engine that canvasses the entire Web, like Google or a metasearch service like DogPile.

It may also help to brush up on "boolean logic," a search language named for 19th century mathematician George Boole who first reduced logical reasoning to mathematical formulas. Not all search engines use Boolean, but many of them offer a form of this logic-based search technique on their "advanced search" pages.

Many search engines work most efficiently when you search using BOOLEAN operators. Don't worry, this is less complicated than it sounds. You just need to become comfortable with using 'and' to combine words, 'or' to split them, quotation marks to search whole phrases, and parentheses to make your search more sophisticated. Here are some examples:

- botany and Indiana: This will bring up all entries that contain both the words botany and Indiana. Use this if you're looking only for Indiana colleges with botany majors.

- botany or Indiana: This will bring up all entries that contain either the word botany or the word Indiana. Use this if you're looking for any college with a botany major, or any college in Indiana.

- botany and (Indiana or Michigan): This will bring up all entries that contain the words botany with the word Indiana or with the word Michigan. Use this if you're looking for schools in either Indiana or Michigan that offer botany majors.

- "field hockey": This will bring up all entries that contain the words field and hockey next to each other, and in that order (instead of looking for the word 'field' in some places and 'hockey' in others). Use this if you're looking for all schools with field hockey teams.

- "field hockey" and (Indiana or Michigan): This will bring up all entries that contain the words "field hockey" with the word Indiana or with the word Michigan. Use this if you're looking only for schools in Indiana or Michigan with field hockey teams.

## How do I search a page full of text?

If you are on a page full of text and you are looking for a specific word, pull down the "edit" menu on your browser. Click on "find" and a window will open where you may type in your word. (If you are using Windows, try Control-F.) Hit enter and the browser will find the word on that page and highlight it for you. Unfortunately, more and more Web pages are using new organizing tools, like frames and scroll bars, that often prevent you from searching everything in an entire Web page at one time. But for Web pages that long documents of text, word searching is still a good option.

## I clicked on a link that doesn't work. Why is that?

If you click on a hyperlink and get an error message, several different things may be happening—none of which you can really control.

- First, the person who constructed the site might have accidentally introduced a typo into the URL. Your browser, then, is searching for a link that doesn't exist and will tell you so. If this happens, your only recourse is to send a message to the site administrator (often known as a Webmaster), alerting him or her of the problem, and hope that it is corrected soon.

- Second, the site behind the link might have moved. This means the code for that particular link is outdated and needs to be corrected with the new URL. Again, there is no easy way out of these dead ends. One suggestion is to delete everything in the address except for the domain name. In other words, if the URL is www.site.com/lookhere1/lookhere2.html, the specific path may have changed. Go to www.site.com and look through the site index. If that doesn't work, send a message about the problem to the site's Webmaster.

- Third, the site's server may be down. In basic terms, this means the computer that holds all the site's files has lost its connection to the Internet. There is nothing you can do about this except try again later.

- And last, the Internet just might be very busy, making all connections sluggish. Connecting to sites in different countries can take a long time as well. If you don't have the patience to wait for a site to load—and I don't blame you—hit the "STOP" BUTTON on your browser and try a different URL.

## My browser continues to reload the same old page, even though I've asked for a new one.

This happens on old browsers—and is probably because your CACHE is full. What is a cache? It's an area on your hard drive that saves copies of the pages and graphics you have loaded onto your browser. That way, when you return to a page you have already visited, the browser does not have to point all the way back to the site to find the page. It can simply retrieve it from your hard drive.

But that cache can fill up. And when it does, the browser gets confused and fails to retrieve new pages for you. To fix the problem, go to the "options" menu on your browser and ask it to empty the cache (On AOL, go to keyword Preferences, then click on WWW Preferences).

## What are plug-ins? Where do I get them?

Plug-ins are utilities that can be added—or "plugged" in—to your browser, enabling it to display many file types beyond simple HTML-coded pages. To see VIDEO, listen to SOUND, and DOWNLOAD software, you usually need a plug-in. The latest browsers have popular plug-ins already installed, so you don't have to do anything. But if you have come across a Web site that requires a plug-in that is not found on your computer, you may need to jump through the hoops to install it.

Installing plug-ins becomes easier after you've done a few, but in the beginning, the process can be harrowing. Since you're adding new software to your computer, you will need to make sure your machine has enough memory to handle the plug-in. You will also be working within the directory of your computer, which is called the "file manager" in early Windows operating systems and "Windows Explorer" in Windows 95, 98 and 2000. On Macs, using plug-ins is less of a hassle, because the desktop is equipped to graphically show you where files are going. When you come to a Web site that requires a plug-in, you will get a message telling you that you will need to install one. Usually, the site will point you to a page that contains links to the one you need. Follow the directions carefully, and for safety's sake, save and close all the files you might be working on at the time.

The plug-in will usually be saved to a temporary folder in your computer. Most advanced browsers automatically take note that the plug-in has been installed, but you will need to shut down and restart the browser to use it.

## What does "download" mean? How do I do it?

When you are downloading a file or piece of software, you are saving that file or software to your hard drive. The plug-ins described above have been downloaded from sites on the Web.

Many electronic applications for college-bound students must be downloaded before they can be used. When you come to a page that asks you to download a file, be prepared to save all your work and reboot your computer. Also, be prepared to wait a while. Depending on the size of the downloadable file, this process can take anywhere from a few minutes to a few hours. Be aware of what your computer can handle. Most electronic applications, fortunately, are not so huge that they require much waiting. Games and videos, however, can take much longer.

When you start to download a file, you might get a message telling you that you need to install a plug-in first. Go to the above section on plug-ins to figure out what you need to do.

When you are ready to download the file, follow the directions closely. Most of the sites mentioned in this book are very good about describing what you need to do. Before you begin, you may want to PRINT THE DIRECTIONS so you can read them even after you have closed your browser and rebooted your computer. Downloaded files are usually saved to a temporary directory on your hard drive by your online service or browser. Look for a folder called "temp" or "download."

In that folder you will see a file that usually says "setup.exe." Click on that file and the installation will begin. From here on out, breathe a sigh of relief. The process is usually very easy and self-explanatory. The file will show up as an icon on your desktop once the process is complete. Click on that icon and the electronic application will appear.

For more on downloading, go to wp.netscape.com/download.

### What if I'm still having problems?

Ideally, you should ask someone in your family or neighborhood who is familiar with computers for help. Each computer has its own quirks— and trouble shooting is easiest when done by someone who knows the type of computer you are using.

If you are using an online service or ISP, call customer service. Sometimes you have to spend time on hold, but the staff should be able to help you. You may also find answers at an online help area, such as the AOL Computing Channel (keyword: computing) or CompuServe's Customer Service Help Database ("go" to "cshelp"). Otherwise, try your local library for general books devoted to using the Internet. They contain more advice than can be provided here, and they offer specific tips for your computer.

The Web, as well, provides help. Try the Netscape home page at www.netscape.com, the Microsoft home page at www.microsoft.com or your online service's Internet section.

### Are there any good Internet sites for "newbies"?

Still confused? While bookstores are loaded with dictionaries and "how-to" books, not surprisingly, you can also find them on line, free.

**Newbies Anonymous: A Newcomer's
Guide to the Internet**
www.geocities.com/TheTropics/1945/index1.htm

**Folks Online: For the World's Non-Technical Majority**
www.folksonline.com

**Internet Glossaries**
www.netlingo.com
www.netdictionary.com

**Netiquette**
www.albion.com/netiquette

**Net M@nners**
www.netmanners.com

GOOD LUCK,
AND HAPPY SURFING!

# INDICES

# Appendix 3
# An Index to Every Internet Address in this Book

| Name | Address (URLs, etc.) | What's Inside |
| --- | --- | --- |
| **Getting Plugged In** | | |
| The List | www.thelist.com | List of Internet Service Providers |
| Google Groups | groups.google.com | Access to newsgroups |
| Mozilla Thunderbird | www.mozilla.org/projects/thunderbird | Access to newsgroups |
| Wi-Fi Hotspots | www.openwifispots.com | List of Wi-Fi Hotspots |
| **Collecting Information About Colleges** | | |
| COOL's Web search | nces.ed.gov/ipeds/cool | Database of college descriptions |
| Peterson's College Search | www.petersons.com | Database of college descriptions |
| College Board Search | www.collegeboard.com | Database of college descriptions |
| Princeton Review's Counselor-O-Matic | www.princetonreview.com/college | Database of college descriptions |
| XAP's Mentor Web Sites | www.xap.com/gotocollege | Database of college descriptions |
| Best College Picks, from Peterson's | www.bestcollegepicks.com | Database of college descriptions |
| CollegeNET Search | www.collegenet.com | Database of college descriptions |
| Find Your Ideal School, by U.S. News | www.usnews.com/usnews/edu/college/tools/search.php | Database of college descriptions |
| Careers and Colleges | www.careersandcolleges.com | Database of college descriptions |
| The College Guide | www.mycollegeguide.org | Database of college descriptions |
| CollegeView Search | www.collegeview.com/collegesearch/index.jsp | Database of college descriptions |
| **Looking for Specific Types of Schools** | | |
| HBCU Connect | www.hbcuconnect.com | Browsable information on historically black colleges |
| Hillel | www.hillel.org | Browsable information on Hillel at US Colleges |
| Jesuit Colleges | www.ajcunet.edu | Browsable information on Jesuit colleges |
| Studyabroad.com | www.studyabroad.com | Browsable information on study-abroad programs |
| CIEE | ciee.org/study.aspx | Browsable information on study-abroad programs |
| Collegeabroad.com | www.collegeabroad.com | Browsable information on study-abroad programs |

| Name | Address (URLs, etc.) | What's inside |
|---|---|---|
| **Finding and Using to College Home Pages** | | |
| YAHOO!'s College Listings—United States | dir.yahoo.com/Education/Higher_Education/ Colleges_and_Universities | Links to home pages of colleges in the U.S. |
| All About College | www.allaboutcollege.com | Links to home pages of colleges around the world |
| U.S. Universities and Community Colleges | www.utexas.edu/world/univ | Links to home pages of colleges in the U.S. |
| Foundation for Independent Higher Education | www.fihe.org/tools/map.asp | Links to home pages of private colleges |
| Canadian Colleges | www.uwaterloo.ca/canu/index.html | Links to home pages of Canadian colleges |
| Community College Web | www.mcli.dist.maricopa.edu/cc | Links to home pages of two-year colleges |
| Community College Finder | www.aacc.nche.edu | Links to home pages of two-year colleges |
| ALLSchools | www.allschools.com | Links to home pages of colleges in the U.S. |
| Professional and Graduate Schools | www.gradschools.com/search.html | Links to home pages of graduate schools |
| Women's College Coalition | www.womenscolleges.org | Links to home pages of women's colleges |
| American Indian Higher Education Consortium | www.aihec.org/colleges.html | Links to home pages of tribal colleges |
| Hispanic Association of American Colleges | www.hacu.net | Links to home pages of Hispanic-Serving Institutions |
| **Getting the Latest College News** | | |
| U-Wire | www.uwire.com | Links to top stories from student newspapers |
| College News Online | www.collegenews.com | Links to top stories from student newspapers |
| News Link | www.newslink.org/statcamp.html | Links to newspapers around the country |
| Inside Higher Education | insidehighered.com | News about higher education |
| Chronicle of Higher Education | chronicle.com | News about higher education |
| Education News | www.topix.net/education | News about higher education |
| National Association for College Admission Counseling | www.nacacnet.org | News about higher education |
| **Getting the Regional Scoop** | | |
| Houston Area Higher Education Resources | www.chron.com/content/community/higher_ed/index.html | Information about colleges in the Houston area |
| The New York Times' Education Coverage | www.nytimes.com/pages/education.html | Information about colleges in NY and elsewhere |
| Los Angeles Times' Education Coverage | www.latimes.com/education | Information about colleges in Southern California |
| The Washington Post's Education Coverage | washingtonpost.com/wp-dyn/education/content/education | Information about colleges in Washington, DC |
| **Thinking About Safety** | | |
| Security on Campus, Inc. | www.securityoncampus.org | Information about crime on campus |

| Name | Address (URLs, etc.) | What's Inside |
|---|---|---|
| **What About College Rankings?** | | |
| U.S. News & World Report | www.usnews.com/sections/education | College rankings |
| Princeton Review's 366 Best Colleges | www.princetonreview.com/college/research/rankings/rankings.asp | |
| Maclean's University Rankings | www.macleans.ca/universities | Colleges ranked by students |
| Laissaez-Faire Rankings | collegeadmissions.tripod.com | Canadian college rankings |
| College Ranking Service | www.rankyourcollege.com | Colleges ranked by selectivity criteria |
| College and University Rankings | www.library.uiuc.edu/edx/rankings.htm | College rankings, tongue-in-cheek |
| | | Comprehensive site about college rankings |
| Evaluating Information Technology on Campus | www.educause.edu/StudentGuideto1T/873 | Questions to ask about campus technology |
| **Preparing for a Campus Tour** | | |
| College Board on College Visits | www.collegeboard.com/student/csearch/college-visits/index.html | Thinking about location |
| CitySearch | www.citysearch.com | Research your future hometown |
| MapQuest | www.mapquest.com | Get directions to college campuses |
| **Taking a Campus Tour—Virtually** | | |
| eCampusTours | www.ecampustours.com | Index of virtual tours |
| The U | www.theu.com | Virtual tours |
| CampusTours.com | www.campustours.com | Index of virtual tours |
| Collegiate Choice Walking Tours | www.collegiatechoice.com | Catalog of indepth videos of campus walking tours |
| **Gathering More Advice** | | |
| Starting Points for Parents and Students | www.collegeboard.com | Guidance on college selection |
| About.Com's College-Admission Guide | collegeapps.about.com | Human guidance on admissions |
| College Comparison Worksheet | www.usnews.com/sections/education | Online worksheet |
| College QuickFinder: Compare | apps.collegeboard.com/search/sidebyside.jsp | Online worksheet |
| College Personality Quiz | www.usnews.com/usnews/edu/college/articles/extras/personality-quiz_brief.php | |
| Dear Admissions Guru... | www.mycollegeguide.org/Guru.php | Online worksheet |
| Getting Ready for University | www.campusaccess.com | Occasional articles on selecting a college |
| Princeton Review's Eye on Apply | www.princetonreview.com/college/apply/eyeonapply/2007/default.asp | Essay on how to choose the right college |
| | | Online tour through the admission process |

| Name | Address (URLs, etc.) | What's Inside |
|---|---|---|
| Facebook | www.facebook.com | Social networking site |
| MySpace | www.myspace.com | Social networking site |
| Xanga | www.xanga.com | Social networking site |
| Friendster | www.friendster.com | Social networking site |
| U.S. News's College Forums | www.usnews.com/sections/education | The most vexing questions |
| Princeton Review's Forums | discuss.princetonreview.com | Online discussions about choosing a college |
| **Do Some Interviews of Your Own** | | |
| The Daily Jolt | www.dailyjolt.com | Links to student forums and home pages |
| **Learning About Distance Education** | | |
| Council for Higher Education Accreditation | www.chea.org | Directory of accrediting agencies |
| Distance Education and Training Council | www.detc.org | Directory of accredited distance ed programs |
| World Wide Learn | www.worldwidelearn.com | Directory of online courses and programs |
| Peterson's Distance Learning | www.petersons.com/distancelearning | Directory of online courses and programs |
| Yahoo's Overview of Distance Education | degrees.education.yahoo.com | Overview of distance education opportunities |
| Online School Guide | www.directoryofschools.com | Catalog of online courses |
| DANTES | www.dantes.doded.mil | Catalog of online courses |
| Virtual University Gazette | www.geteducated.com/vug/index.asp | Electronic newsletter on distance education |
| DegreeNet | www.degree.net | Background information on distance education |
| **A Sampling of Distance-Ed Programs** | | |
| University of Phoenix | www.phoenix.edu | Online business education |
| Western Governors University | www.wgu.edu | Virtual university |
| Capella University | www.capellauniversity.edu | Accredited online university |
| Jones International University | www.jonesinternational.edu | Accredited Online university |
| Online Learning at Parkland College | online.parkland.edu | Links to online course providers, and courses |
| CIC Course Share | www.cic.net/AcademicCollaboration.shtml | Online education at Big 10 Schools |
| New School Online University | online.newschool.edu | Online undergrad degree offered by New School |
| Servicemembers Opportunity College | www.soc.aascu.org | Online degrees for servicemembers and their families |
| Southern Regional Electronic Campus | www.electroniccampus.org | Online education at southern universities |
| SUNY Learning Network | sln.suny.edu | Online education at State University of NY schools |

| Name | Address (URLs, etc.) | What's Inside |
|---|---|---|
| **Cooperative Education** | | |
| National Commission for Cooperative Education | www.northeastern.edu/co-op | Online guide to co-op |
| Cooperative Education Association | www.ceiainc.org | Links to co-op sites |
| Co-op Student Handbook | www.northeastern.edu/co-op | Online guide to co-op |
| Studentjobs.gov | www.studentjobs.gov | Cooperative Education with the Federal Government |
| **Those Stressful Standardized Tests** | | |
| About the SAT | www.collegeboard.com/student/testing/sat/about.html | Overview of the New SAT |
| SAT Dates and Fees | www.collegeboard.com/student/testing/sat/calenfees.html | Standardized testing information |
| Online SAT Registration | www.collegeboard.com/student/testing/sat/reg.html | Standardized testing information |
| Educational Testing Service Network | www.ets.org | Standardized testing information |
| ACT's Web site | www.actstudent.org | Standardized testing information |
| ACT Assessment Test Dates | www.actstudent.org/regist/currentdates.html | Standardized testing information |
| Registering for the ACT Assessment | www.actstudent.org/regist | Standardized testing information |
| Wordsmyth S.A.T. Dictionary | www.lightlink.com/bobp/wedt/sat.htm | Dictionary of words that appear on SAT |
| Number2.com | www.number2.com | Free, online prep |
| Kaplan's Test Prep | www.kaptest.com | Online test prep |
| Peterson's Test Prep | www.petersons.com | Online test prep |
| Princeton Review | www.princetonreview.com/college/testPrep | Online test prep |
| College Power Prep | www.powerprep.com | Online test prep |
| Study Hall | www.studyhall.com | Online test prep |
| College Board's SAT Preparation Center | www.collegeboard.com/student/testing/sat | Online test prep |
| Apex Learning—Online Courses for AP Exams | www.apexlearning.com | Online AP courses |
| AP Help from the College Board | www.collegeboard.com/student/testing/ap/about.html | Info about AP tests |
| AP Credit Policy Information | apps.collegeboard.com/apcreditpolicy/index.jsp | Info about colleges' AP credit policy |
| **Online Applications** | | |
| CollegeNET's ApplyWeb Online Applications | www.applyweb.com | Online applications |
| XAP Applications | www.xap.com/apply | Online applications |
| Next Stop College | www.collegeboard.com/student/apply | Online applications |
| The Common Application | app.commonapp.org | Direct link to the electronic Common Application |
| Universal College Application | www.universalcollegeapp.com | Direct link to the electronic Universal College App |
| Zinch | www.zinch.com | Create an online profile |

| Name | Address (URLs, etc.) | What's Inside |
|---|---|---|
| **Ugh! The Essay** | | |
| IvyEssays | www.ivyessays.com | Free advice and fee-based essay services |
| EssayEdge | www.essayedge.com | Free advice and fee-based essay services |
| Cambridge Essay Service | www.hbsguru.com | Free advice and fee-based essay services |
| **Useful References For Any Writer** | | |
| Wordsmyth Educational Dictionary-Thesaurus | www.wordsmyth.net | Online dictionary |
| Thesaurus | www.thesaurus.com | Online version of Roget's Thesaurus |
| Dictionary | www.dictionary.com | Online dictionary |
| The Slot | www.theslot.com | Online style manual |
| The Elements of Style | www.bartleby.com | The classic guide to effective writing |
| **Don't Forget the Interview** | | |
| Princeton Review's interview advice | www.princetonreview.com/college/research/articleindex.asp | Interview advice |
| College Admissions Office E-mail Addresses | www.college-scholarships.com | Links to admission offices' E-mail addresses |
| **Dealing with Recommendations** | | |
| Secondary School Report Form | www.nacacnet.org/MemberPortal/products/forms.html | For guidance counselors |
| Princeton Review's Advice on Recommendations | www.princetonreview.com/college/research/articleindex.asp | Getting better recommendations |
| **Financial Aid—Thinking Ahead** | | |
| Kiplinger's Personal Finance Magazine | www.kiplinger.com | Investing for college |
| Money Magazine | www.money.cnn.com/pf/101/lessons/11 | Investing for college |
| SmartMoney Magazine | www.smartmoney.com/college | Investing for college |
| Financial Aid Calculators | www.finaid.org/calculators | Fifteen calculators designed for college planning |
| College Board's Financial Aid Services | www.collegeboard.com/student/pay | Information about saving for college |
| Fidelity | www.fidelity.com | Investment advice |
| Morningstar | www.morningstar.com | Investment advice |
| Vanguard | www.vanguard.com | Investment advice |
| The Street | www.thestreet.com | Investment advice |
| Quicken | www.quicken.com | Investment advice |
| The Motley Fool | www.fool.com | Investment advice |

| Name | Address (URLs, etc.) | What's inside |
|---|---|---|
| **Financial Aid 101** | | |
| FinAid! The Smart Student's Guide to Financial Aid | www.finaid.org | Information on loans, scholarships, and scams |
| Students.Gov | www.students.gov | Department of Education's central student aid site |
| College is Possible | www.collegeispossible.org | About college planning |
| CollegeAnswer | www.collegeanswer.com | About loans |
| Mapping Your Future | www.mapping-your-future.org/paying | About paying for college |
| California Student Aid Commission | www.csac.ca.gov | About paying for college |
| California Student Aid Commission | www.edfund.org | About paying for college |
| Illinois Student Assistance Commission | www.collegezone.org | About paying for college |
| Texas Guaranteed Student Loan Corporation | www.tgslc.org | About paying for college |
| Texas Guaranteed Student Loan Corporation | www.AdventuresinEducation.org | About paying for college |
| **Applying for Financial Aid** | | |
| Expected Family Contribution calculator | www.collegeboard.com/student/pay | Calculator for figuring out your EFC |
| FAFSA on the Web | www.fafsa.ed.gov | Web-based version of the FAFSA |
| Personal Identification Number | www.pin.ed.gov | Apply for a personal identification number |
| FAFSA-4-Caster | www.fafsa4caster.ed.gov | Preview your EFC |
| PROFILE | profileonline.collegeboard.com | PROFILE Registration and Q-and-A |
| **Federal Student Aid** | | |
| Funding Education Beyond High School | studentaid.ed.gov | The government's guide to federal student aid |
| Office of Postsecondary Education | www.ed.gov/about/offices/list/OPE/index.html | Technical resources from the Dept. of Education |
| Financial Aid Letters | www.financialaidletters.com | Decoding your financial aid letter |
| **Federal Student Loans** | | |
| Direct Loan Program | www.ed.gov/DirectLoan | Government information on direct lending |
| SimpleTuition | www.simpletuition.com | Compare lenders |
| eStudentLoan | www.estudentloan.com | Compare lenders |
| Sallie Mae | www.salliemae.com | Information on loans and the company itself |
| **Banks, Guaranty Agencies, and More** | | |
| Yahoo's List of Lenders | dir.yahoo.com/Education/Financial_Aid/Loans | Links to sites maintained by lenders |
| Access Group | www.accessgroup.org | Source for federal student loans |

| Name | Address (URLs, etc.) | What's Inside |
| --- | --- | --- |
| ASAP/Union Bank and Trust | www.asapubt.com | Source for federal student loans |
| Bank of America | www.bankofamerica.com/studentbanking | Source for federal student loans |
| Chase | www.educationone.com | Source for federal student loans |
| Chase | www.studentloannet.com | Source for federal student loans |
| Chela Education Financing | www.chelastudentloans.org | Source for federal student loans |
| Citibank | www.studentloan.com | Source for federal student loans |
| College Loan Corporation | www.collegeloan.com | Source for federal student loans |
| Key Education Resources | www.key.com/education | Source for federal student loans |
| LoanStar Student Program | www.loanstar.com | Source for federal student loans |
| National City | www.nationalcity.com | Source for federal student loans |
| PNC Bank | www.eduloans.pncbank.com | Source for federal student loans |
| Southwest Student Services | www.sssc.com | Source for federal student loans |
| Student Loan Funding | www.studentloanfunding.org | Source for federal student loans |
| SunTrust Bank | www.suntrusteducation.com | Source for federal student loans |
| US Bank | www.usbank.com/studentloans | Source for federal student loans |
| Wachovia | www.wachovia.com/personal | Source for federal student loans |
| Wells Fargo | wellsfargo.com/per/accounts/student | Source for federal student loans |
| LoanLocator | www.nslc.org | Track your student loans |
| State Guaranty Agencies | wdcrobcolp01.ed.gov/Programs/EROD/org_list.cfm | List of state loan guaranty agencies |

**Tax Cuts Explained**

| Name | Address (URLs, etc.) | What's Inside |
| --- | --- | --- |
| IRS Tax Information for Students | www.irs.gov/individuals/students/index.html | Information about education tax benefits from the IRS |
| Tax Benefits for Education | www.irs.gov/pub/irs-pdf/p970.pdf | Information about education tax benefits for students |
| The Motley Fool | www.fool.com/taxes/taxcenter | Information about tax planning |
| Kiplinger Tax Center | www.kiplinger.com/taxcenter | Information about tax planning |

**State-Based Student Aid**

| Name | Address (URLs, etc.) | What's Inside |
| --- | --- | --- |
| State Education Agencies | wdcrobcolp01.ed.gov/Programs/EROD/org_list.cfm | Links to state-specific sites on financial aid |
| State Grant Agencies | wdcrobcolp01.ed.gov/Programs/EROD/org_list.cfm | Links to state-specific sites on financial aid |
| State Higher-Education Agencies | wdcrobcolp01.ed.gov/Programs/EROD/org_list.cfm | Links to state-specific sites on financial aid |
| College Savings Plans Network | www.collegesavings.org | Directory of state-based college savings plans |
| Internet Guide to "529" Plans | www.savingforcollege.com | Comparison of state-based college savings plans |

| Name | Address (URLs, etc.) | What's Inside |
|---|---|---|
| **Collegiate-Based Student Aid** | | |
| Financial Aid Office Web Pages | www.finaid.org/otheraid/fao.phtml | Links to colleges' financial-aid offices |
| College Aid Offices | www.yahoo.com/Education/Financial_Aid | Links to colleges' financial-aid offices |
| **Focusing on Scholarships** | | |
| FastWeb | www.fastWeb.com | Personalized scholarship-search service |
| MACH25 | www.collegenet.com/mach25 | Personalized scholarship-search service |
| ExPAN Scholarship Search | www.collegeboard.org/student/pay | Scholarship-search service |
| CollegeAnswer (from Sallie Mae) | www.collegeanswer.com | Database of scholarship programs |
| Pacific NW Scholarship Guide | www.collegeplan.org/cpnow/pnwguide/pnwguide.htm | Scholarship-search service for Pacific NW students |
| Scholarship Research Network | www.smexpress.com | Scholarship-search service |
| United Negro College Fund | www.uncf.org | Scholarships typically for minority students |
| Gates Millenium Scholarship Program | www.gmsp.org | Scholarship fund for low-income minority students |
| Black Excel | www.blackexcel.org/link4.htm | Browse scholarship services for minority students |
| American Society of Association Executives | www.asaenet.org | Links to 1700 associations on the Web |
| Foundation Center | www.fdncenter.org/funders | Links to private foundations |
| **Don't Get Scammed** | | |
| Scholarship Scams | www.ftc.gov/bcp/conline/edcams/scholarship | Tips on spotting scams |
| Evaluating Scholarship Matching Services | www.finaid.org/scholarships/matching.phtml | Protecting yourself from scams |
| **Considering the Military** | | |
| Military.com | education.military.com/education-home | Information on military programs and careers |
| ROTC Headquarters | www.defenselink.mil/faq/pis/19.html | Information on ROTC |
| GI Bill Web Site | www.gibill.va.gov | Information on the GI Bill |
| My (Military) Future | www.myfuture.com | Information on ROTC and other military programs |
| **Considering Community Service** | | |
| Americorps | www.americorps.gov | Information on AmeriCorps |
| Corporation for National Service | www.nationalservice.org | Information on National Service |
| Presidential Freedom Scholars | www.learnandserve.gov/about/programs/pfs.asp | Information on Presidential Freedom Awards |
| CityYear | www.cityyear.org | Information on City-Year's service programs |

| Name | Address (URLs, etc.) | What's Inside |
|---|---|---|
| **For Future Health Professionals** | | |
| National Health Service Corps | nhsc.bhpr.hrsa.gov | Federal money for soon-to-be nurses and doctors |
| Bureau of Health Professions | www.hrsa.gov/help/healthprofessions.htm | Federal money for soon-to-be nurses and doctors |
| **If You're an Athlete** | | |
| NCAA Guide for College-Bound Student-Athletes | www.ncaa.org | NCAA guide to scholarships, recruiting, and eligibility |
| NCAA Initial Eligibility Clearinghouse | www.ncaaclearinghouse.net | NCAA's academic eligibility clearinghouse |
| NJCAA Guide for Athletes | www.njcaa.org | Sports programs at Junior Colleges |
| Campus Champs | www.campuschamps.com | Summary of athletic opportunities |
| Women's Sports Foundation | www.womenssportsfoundation.org | Sports information for women |
| Scout USA | www.scoutusa.com | Recruiting service |
| Athletes Advisor | www.athletesadvisor.com | Recruiting service |
| Prepstar | prepstar.com | Recruiting service |
| College Prospects of America | www.cpoa.com | Recruiting service |
| College Bound Student Alliance | www.cbsa.com | Recruiting service |
| National Directory of College Athletics | www.collegiatedirectories.com | E-mail addresses for college coaches |
| **Commercial Education Loans** | | |
| eStudent Loan | www.estudentloan.com | Side by side comparison of private loans |
| The Education Resources Institute | www.teri.org | Source for private loans |
| Nellie Mae | www.nelliemae.com | Source for private loans |
| NextStudent | www.nextstudent.com | Source for private loans |
| GATE | www.gateloan.com | Source for private loans |
| International Education Finance Corporation | www.IEFC.com | Source for private loans for study abroad |
| **Installment Plans** | | |
| TuitionPay | www.tuitionpay.com | Administers monthly-payment plans |
| Tuition Management Systems | www.afford.com | Administers monthly-payment plans |
| **A Few More Radical Options** | | |
| UPromise | www.upromise.com | Investment program for parents |
| Sage Tuition Rewards Program | www.sagescholars.com | Investment program for parents |
| My Rich Uncle | www.myrichuncle.com | Loan alternative |

| Name | Address (URLs, etc.) | What's Inside |
|---|---|---|
| BabyMint | www.babymint.com | Investment program for parents |
| FutureTrust | www.futuretrust.com | Investment program for parents |
| College Rewards MasterCard | www.fidelity.com | Investment program and credit card for parents |
| College Tuition Match | www.collegetuitionmatch.com | Bid on college tuition |
| **Second Chances** | | |
| Annual Student Vacancy Survey | www.nebhe.org/vacancy_survey.html | Survey of colleges in New England with openings |
| NACAC Space Availability Survey | www.nacacnet.org/MemberPortal | Survey of NACAC colleges with openings |
| **Cyber-College Life (in ABC order)** | | |
| #1 Free Stuff | www.1freestuff.com | Free stuff on the web |
| Black Collegian Online | www.black-collegian.com | Articles, chat rooms, and links to college life sites |
| Campus Access | www.campusaccess.com | Articles, essays |
| Campus Circle | www.campuscircle.net | Online source for college entertainment |
| CampusEstore.com | www.campusestore.com | Discounts for students |
| College Club | www.collegeclub.com | Articles, chat rooms, and links to college life sites |
| Collegiate Standard | www.collegiatestandard.com | Articles, essays |
| DORM Store | www.dormtours.net/eshop.asp | An online shop tailored for college-bound students |
| GreekChat | www.greekchat.com | Articles, links on fraternity and sorority life |
| GreekPages | www.greekpages.com | Articles and links to sites about greek life |
| Internet Guide to Spring Break | www.springbreak.com | Links to information on spring break |
| mtvU | www.mtvu.com | Segments on college life |
| Pick-a-Prof | www.pick-a-prof.com | Faculty evaluations |
| Roomate Service.com | www.roommates.com | Roommate matching service |
| StudentAdvantage.Com | www.studentadvantage.com | Discounts, articles, tools |
| Student Center | www.student.com | Articles, chat rooms, and links to college life sites |
| Student Counseling Virtual Pamphlet Collection | www.dr-bob.org/vpc | Links to virtual pamphlets on counseling topics |
| U Magazine from Colleges.com | www.colleges.com/umagazine/index.html | Articles, chat and tools |
| Universal Black Pages | www.ubp.com | Articles and links to sites about HBCUs |
| Google's list of e-zines | www.google.com/Top/News/Colleges_and_Universities/ Magazines_and_E-zines | Links to more college-life magazines |
| Yahoo!'s list of e-zines | dir.yahoo.com/News_and_Media/College_and_University/ Magazines | Links to more college-life magazines |

| Name | Address (URLs, etc.) | What's Inside |
|---|---|---|
| **E-Campus Bookstores and Online Class Notes** | | |
| Best Book Buys | www.bestbookbuys.com | Searches online bookstores for best buys |
| EFollett | www.Efollet.com | Online source for college textbooks |
| Varsity Books | www.varsitybooks.com | Online source for college textbooks |
| Big Words | www.bigwords.com | Online source for college textbooks |
| E Campus | www.ecampus.com | Online source for college textbooks |
| ClassBook | www.classbook.com | Online source for used college textbooks |
| MIT OpenCourseWare | ocw.mit.edu | Online class notes for MIT |
| Utah State's OpenCourseWare | ocw.usu.edu | Online class notes for Utah State |
| Notre Dame's OpenCourseWare | ocw.nd.edu | Online class notes for Notre Dame |
| Tufts' OpenCourseWare | ocw.tufts.edu | Online class notes for Tufts University |
| Johns Hopkins School of Public Health | ocw.jhsph.edu | Online class notes for Johns Hopkins |
| Open Coursework Consortium | ocwconsortium.org | Index of schools offering online class notes |
| Turn It In | www.turnitin.com | Site to help professors catch online plagiarists |
| Plagiarism.org | www.plagiarism.org | Site to help professors catch online plagiarists |
| Essay Verification Engine (EVE) | www.canexus.com/eve | Site to help professors catch online plagiarists |
| **Metasites (In ABC order)** | | |
| About.Com's College Admission page | collegeapps.about.com | Human guidance, links, Q-and-A |
| America Online's College Planning Areas | Keyword: College | Searches, links, chats, Financial planning, more |
| Black Excel | www.blackexcel.org | Financial aid, advice for black college-bound student |
| Careers and Colleges | www.careersandcolleges.com | Searches, Q-and-A areas, and more |
| CollegeAnswer from Sallie Mae | www.collegeanswer.com | Searches, Q-and-A areas, and more |
| College Board Online | www.collegeboard.com | Searches, Q-and-A areas, and more |
| College Confidential | www.collegeconfidential.com | Searches, Q-and-A areas, and more |
| CollegeNET | www.collegenet.com | Searches, Q-and-A areas, and more |
| College Planning | www.collegeplan.org | Searches, Advice, and more |
| College Prep 101 | collegeprep.okstate.edu | Searches, Articles, and more |
| College Solutions Network | www.csnamerica.com | Searches, Articles, Test Prep and more |
| CollegeView | www.collegeview.com | Searches, Q-and-A areas, and more |
| FinAid Page | www.finaid.org | Financial-aid guides, Q-and-A areas, and more |
| Go College | www.gocollege.com | Scholarship news, and more |
| Guidance On Line | home.cfl.rr.com/nwunder/guidance.html | Advice, links, and more |
| My College Guide | www.mycollegeguide.org | Searches, Articles, and more |

| Name | Address (URLs, etc.) | What's Inside |
|------|---------------------|---------------|
| MyRoad.com | myroad.collegeboard.com/myroad/navigator.jsp | Searches, Career Information, and more |
| NACAC | www.nacacnet.org/MemberPortal/News/stepsnewsletter | News and more |
| Peterson's Education Portal | www.petersons.com | Searches, Q-and-A areas, and more |
| Princeton Review | www.princetonreview.com | Searches, Articles, Test Prep and more |
| ScholarStuff | www.scholarstuff.com | Searches, Q-and-A areas, and more |
| **Getting Ready for Graduate School** | | |
| Student Doctor Network | www.studentdoctor.net | Searches, Articles, Advice and more for Pre-meds |
| Find Law for Law Students | stu.findlaw.com/prelaw | Searches, Articles, Advice and more for Pre-laws |
| Internet Legal Resource Guide | www.ilrg.com/pre-law.html | Searches, Articles, Advice and more for Pre-laws |
| Law Jobs and Career Center | www.law.com/jsp/law/careercenter/index.jsp | Searches, Articles, Advice and more for Pre-laws |
| MBA Pathfinder | www.mba.com | Searches, Articles, Advice and more for Pre-bness |
| **Free E-Mail Services** | | |
| Big Foot | www.bigfoot.com | Commercial e-mail provider |
| CollegeClub | www.collegeclub.com | Commercial e-mail provider |
| Hotmail | www.hotmail.com | Commercial e-mail provider |
| Mail.com | www.mail.com | Commercial e-mail provider |
| Lycos | mail.lycos.com | Commercial e-mail provider |
| Yahoo! | mail.yahoo.com | Commercial e-mail provider |
| Google | gmail.google.com | Commercial e-mail provider |
| Mail2Web | www.mail2web.com | Check e-mail while away from your computer |
| **E-Mail Privacy Services** | | |
| ZixMail | www.zixcorp.com | Privacy enhancements to existing email |
| HushMail.com | www.hushmail.com | Private e-mail accounts |
| **Internet Search Services** | | |
| Google Groups | groups.google.com | Search engine for Usenet newsgroups |
| Google | www.google.com | Search engine and catalog of the Web |
| Google Toolbar | toolbar.google.com | Google toolbar for your desktop |
| Yahoo! | www.yahoo.com | Search engine and catalog of the Web |
| Alltheweb | www.alltheweb.com | Search engine and catalog of the Web |

| Name | Address (URLs, etc.) | What's Inside |
|---|---|---|
| Ask.com | www.ask.com | Search engine and catalog of the Web |
| AltaVista | www.altavista.com | Search engine and catalog of the Web |
| AOL Search | Keyword: search | AOL directory and Web search engine |
| Live | www.live.com | Search engine and directory |
| Lycos | www.lycos.com | Search engine and catalog of the Web |
| **Metasearch Engines** | | |
| Dogpile | www.dogpile.com | Metasearch engine |
| Mamma.com | www.mamma.com | Metasearch engine |
| Search | www.search.com | Metasearch engine |
| Metacrawler | www.metacrawler.com | Metasearch engine |
| **Online Help** | | |
| Information on downloading | wp.netscape.com/download | Online help |
| AOL Computing Channel | Keyword: computing | Online help |
| CompuServe's Customer Service | "go" to "cshelp" | Online help |
| Netscape's home page | www.netscape.com | Online help |
| Microsoft's home page | www.microsoft.com | Online help |
| **Internet Sites for Newbies** | | |
| Newbies Anonymous: A Guide to the Internet | www.geocities.com/TheTropics/1945/index1.htm | An Internet introduction |
| Folks Online: For the World's Non-Technical Majority | www.folksonline.com | An Internet introduction |
| NetLingo | www.netlingo.com | An Internet glossary |
| NetDictionary | www.netdictionary.com | An Internet glossary |
| Netiquette | www.albion.com/netiquette | An introduction to netiquette |
| Net M@nners | www.netmanners.com | An introduction to netiquette |

# Alphabetical Index of Web Sites

| Name | Address (URLs, etc.) | What's inside |
|---|---|---|
| #1 Free Stuff | www.1freestuff.com | Free stuff on the web |
| About.Com's College-Admission Guide | collegeapps.about.com | Human guidance on admissions |
| Access Group | www.accessgroup.org | Source for federal student loans |
| ACT Assessment Test Dates | www.actstudent.org/regist/currentdates.html | Standardized testing information |
| ACT Registration | www.actstudent.org/regist | Standardized testing information |
| ACT's Web site | www.acistudent.org | Standardized testing information |
| All About College | www.allaboutcollege.com | Links to home pages of colleges around the world |
| ALLSchools | www.allschools.com | Links to home pages of colleges in the U.S. |
| Alltheweb | www.alltheweb.com | Search engine and catalog of the Web |
| AltaVista | www.altavista.com | Search engine and catalog of the Web |
| American Indian Higher Education Consortium | www.aihec.org/colleges.html | Links to home pages of tribal colleges |
| American Society of Association Executives | www.asaenet.org | Links to 1700 associations on the Web |
| Americorps | www.americorps.gov | Information on AmeriCorps |
| Annual Student Vacancy Survey | www.nebhe.org/vacancy_survey.html | Survey of colleges in New England with openings |
| AOL Computing Channel | Keyword: computing | Online help |
| AOL Search | Keyword: search | AOL directory and Web search engine |
| AOL's College Planning Areas | Keyword: College | Searches, links, chats, Financial planning, more |
| AP Credit Policy Information | apps.collegeboard.com/apcreditpolicy/index.jsp | Info about colleges' AP credit policy |
| AP Help from the College Board | www.collegeboard.com/student/testing/ap/about.html | Info about AP tests |
| Apex Learning-Online Courses for AP Exams | www.apexlearning.com | Online AP courses |
| ASAP/Union Bank and Trust | www.asapubt.com | Source for federal student loans |
| Ask.com | www.ask.com | Search engine and catalog of the Web |
| Athletes Advisor | www.athletesadvisor.com | Recruiting service |
| BabyMint | www.babymint.com | Investment program for parents |
| Bank of America | www.bankofamerica.com/studentbanking | Source for federal student loans |
| Best Book Buys | www.bestbookbuys.com | Searches online bookstores for best buys |
| Big Foot | www.bigfoot.com | Commercial e-mail provider |
| Big Words | www.bigwords.com | Online source for college textbooks |

| Name | Address (URLs, etc.) | What's inside |
|---|---|---|
| Black Collegian Online | www.black-collegian.com | Articles, chat rooms, and links to college life sites |
| Black Excel | www.blackexcel.org | Financial aid, advice for black college-bound student |
| Bureau of Health Professions | www.hrsa.gov/help/healthprofessions.htm | Federal money for soon-to-be nurses and doctors |
| California Student Aid Commission | www.csac.ca.gov | About paying for college |
| California Student Aid Commission | www.edfund.org | About paying for college |
| Cambridge Essay Service | www.hbsguru.com | Free advice and fee-based essay services |
| Campus Access | www.campusaccess.com | Articles, essays |
| Campus Champs | www.campuschamps.com | Summary of athletic opportunities |
| Campus Circle | www.campuscircle.net | Online source for college entertainment |
| CampusEstore.com | www.campusestore.com | Discounts for students |
| CampusTours.com | www.campustours.com | Index of virtual tours |
| Canadian Colleges | www.uwaterloo.ca/canu/index.html | Links to home pages of Canadian colleges |
| Capella University | www.capellauniversity.edu | Accredited online university |
| Careers and Colleges | www.careersandcolleges.com | Database of college descriptions |
| Chase | www.educationone.com | Source for federal student loans |
| Chase | www.studentloannet.com | Source for federal student loans |
| Chela Education Financing | www.chelastudentloans.org | Source for federal student loans |
| Chronicle of Higher Education | chronicle.com | News about higher education |
| CIC  Course Share | www.cic.net/AcademicCollaboration.shtml | Online education at Big 10 Schools |
| CIEE | ciee.org/study.aspx | Browsable information on study-abroad programs |
| Citibank | www.studentloan.com | Source for federal student loans |
| CitySearch | www.citysearch.com | Research your future hometown |
| CityYear | www.cityyear.org | Information on City-Year's service programs |
| ClassBook | www.classbook.com | Online source for used college textbooks |
| College Admissions Office E-mail Addresses | www.college-scholarships.com | Links to admission offices' E-mail addresses |
| College Aid Offices | www.yahoo.com/Education/Financial_Aid | Links to colleges' financial-aid offices |
| College and University Rankings | www.library.uiuc.edu/edx/rankings.htm | Comprehensive site about college rankings |
| College Board on College Visits | www.collegeboard.com/student/csearch/college-visits/index.html | Thinking about location |
| College Board's Financial Aid Services | www.collegeboard.com/student/pay | Information about saving for college |
| College Board Online | www.collegeboard.com | Searches, Q-and-A areas, and more |
| College Bound Student Alliance | www.cbsa.com | Recruiting service |
| College Club | www.collegeclub.com | Articles, chat rooms, and links to college life sites |
| College Comparison Worksheet | www.usnews.com/sections/education | Online worksheet |
| College Confidential | www.collegeconfidential.com | Searches, Q-and-A areas, and more |

| Name | Address (URLs, etc.) | What's Inside |
|---|---|---|
| College is Possible | www.collegeispossible.org | About college planning |
| College Loan Corporation | www.collegeloan.com | Source for federal student loans |
| College News Online | www.collegenews.com | Links to top stories from student newspapers |
| College Personality Quiz | www.usnews.com/usnews/edu/college/articles/extras/personality-quiz_brief.php | |
| College Planning | www.collegeplan.org | Online worksheet |
| College Power Prep | www.powerprep.com | Searches, Advice, and more |
| College Prep 101 | collegeprep.okstate.edu | Online test prep |
| College Prospects of America | www.cpoa.com | Searches, Articles, and more |
| College QuickFinder: Compare | apps.collegeboard.com/search/sidebyside.jsp | Recruiting service |
| College Ranking Service | www.rankyourcollege.com | Online worksheet |
| College Rewards MasterCard | www.fidelity.com | College rankings, tongue-in-cheek |
| College Savings Plans Network | www.collegesavings.org | Investment program and credit card for parents |
| College Solutions Network | www.csnamerica.com | Directory of state-based college savings plans |
| College Tuition Match | www.collegetuitionmatch.com | Searches, Articles, Test Prep and more |
| Collegeabroad.com | www.collegeabroad.com | Bid on college tuition |
| CollegeAnswer (from Sallie Mae) | www.collegeanswer.com | Browsable information on study-abroad programs |
| CollegeNET | www.collegenet.com | Database of scholarship programs |
| CollegeNET's ApplyWeb Online Applications | www.applyweb.com | Searches, Q-and-A areas, and more |
| CollegeView | www.collegeview.com | Online applications |
| Collegiate Choice Walking Tours | www.collegiatechoice.com | Searches, Q-and-A areas, and more |
| Collegiate Standard | www.collegiatestandard.com | Catalog of indepth videos of campus walking tours |
| Common Application | app.commonapp.org | Articles, essays |
| Community College Finder | www.aacc.nche.edu | Direct link to the electronic Common Application |
| Community College Web | www.mcli.dist.maricopa.edu/cc | Links to home pages of two-year colleges |
| CompuServe's Customer Service | go to "cshelp" | Links to home pages of two-year colleges |
| COOL's Web search | nces.ed.gov/ipeds/cool | Online help |
| Co-op Student Handbook | www.northeastern.edu/co-op | Database of college descriptions |
| Cooperative Education Association | www.ceainc.org | Online guide to co-op |
| Corporation for National Service | www.nationalservice.org | Links to co-op sites |
| Council for Higher Education Accreditation | www.chea.org | Information on National Service |
| | | Directory of accrediting agencies |
| Daily Jolt | www.dailyjolt.com | Links to student forums and home pages |
| DANTES | www.dantes.doded.mil | Catalog of online courses |
| Dear Admissions Guru... | www.mycollegeguide.org/Guru.php | Occasional articles on selecting a college |

| Name | Address (URLs, etc.) | What's Inside |
|---|---|---|
| DegreeNet | www.degree.net | Background information on distance education |
| Dictionary | www.dictionary.com | Online dictionary |
| Direct Loan Program | www.ed.gov/DirectLoan | Government information on direct lending |
| Distance Education and Training Council | www.detc.org | Directory of accredited distance ed programs |
| Dogpile | www.dogpile.com | Metasearch engine |
| DORM Store | www.dormtours.net/eshop.asp | An online shop tailored for college-bound students |
| E Campus | www.ecampus.com | Online source for college textbooks |
| eCampusTours | www.ecampustours.com | Index of virtual tours |
| Educational Testing Service Network | www.ets.org | Standardized testing information |
| EFollett | www.Efollet.com | Online source for college textbooks |
| Essay Verification Engine (EVE) | www.canexus.com/eve | Site to help professors catch online plagiarists |
| EssayEdge | www.essayedge.com | Free advice and fee-based essay services |
| eStudent Loan | www.estudentloan.com | Side by side comparison of private loans |
| Evaluating Information Technology on Campus | www.educause.edu/StudentGuidetoIT/873 | Questions to ask about campus technology |
| Evaluating Scholarship Matching Services | www.finaid.org/scholarships/matching.phtml | Protecting yourself from scams |
| ExPAN Scholarship Search | www.collegeboard.org/student/pay | Scholarship-search service |
| Expected Family Contribution calculator | www.collegeboard.com/student/pay | Calculator for figuring out your EFC |
| Facebook | www.facebook.com | Social networking site |
| FAFSA on the Web | www.fafsa.ed.gov | Web-based version of the FAFSA |
| FAFSA-4-Caster | www.fafsa4caster.ed.gov | Preview your EFC |
| FastWeb | www.fastWeb.com | Personalized scholarship-search service |
| Fidelity | www.fidelity.com | Investment advice |
| FinAid! The Smart Student's Guide to Financial Aid | www.finaid.org | Information on loans, scholarships, and scams |
| Financial Aid Calculators | www.finaid.org/calculators | Fifteen calculators designed for college planning |
| Financial Aid Letters | www.financialaidletters.com | Decoding your financial aid letter |
| Find Law for Law Students | www.finaid.org/otheraid/fao.phtml | Links to colleges' financial-aid offices |
| Folks Online: For the World's Non-Technical Majority | stu.findlaw.com/prelaw | Searches, Articles, Advice and more for Pre-laws |
| Foundation Center | www.folksonline.com | An Internet introduction |
| Foundation for Independent Higher Education | www.fdncenter.org/funders | Links to private foundations |
| Friendster | www.fihe.org/tools/map.asp | Links to home pages of private colleges |
| Funding Education Beyond High School | www.friendster.com | Social networking site |
| FutureTrust | studentaid.ed.gov | The government's guide to federal student aid |
| | www.futuretrust.com | Investment program for parents |

| Name | Address (URLs, etc.) | What's Inside |
|---|---|---|
| GATE | www.gateloan.com | Source for private loans |
| Gates Millenium Scholarship Program | www.gmsp.org | Scholarship fund for low-income minority students |
| GI Bill Web Site | www.gibill.va.gov | Information on the GI Bill |
| Google | www.google.com | Search engine and catalog of the Web |
| Google Groups | groups.google.com | Search engine for Usenet newsgroups |
| Google Mail | gmail.google.com | Commercial e-mail provider |
| Google Toolbar | toolbar.google.com | Google toolbar for your desktop |
| Google's list of e-zines | www.google.com/Top/News/Colleges_and_Universities/ Magazines_and_E-zines | Links to more college-life magazines |
| GreekChat | www.greekchat.com | Articles, links on fraternity and sorority life |
| GreekPages | www.greekpages.com | Articles and links to sites about greek life |
| Guidance On Line | home.cfl.rr.com/nwunder/guidance.html | Advice, links, and more |
| HBCU Connect | www.hbcuconnect.com | Browsable information on historically black colleges |
| Hillel | www.hillel.org | Browsable information on Hillel at US Colleges |
| Hispanic Association of American Colleges | www.hacu.net | Links to home pages of Hispanic-Serving Institutions |
| Hotmail | www.hotmail.com | Commercial e-mail provider |
| Houston Area Higher Education Resources | www.chron.com/content/community/higher_ed/index.html | Information about colleges in the Houston area |
| HushMail.com | www.hushmail.com | Private e-mail accounts |
| Illinois Student Assistance Commission | www.collegezone.org | About paying for college |
| Information on downloading | wp.netscape.com/download | Online help |
| Inside Higher Education | insidehighered.com | News about higher education |
| International Education Finance Corporation | www.IEFC.com | Source for private loans for study abroad |
| Internet Guide to "529" Plan | www.savingforcollege.com | Comparison of state-based college savings plans |
| Internet Guide to Spring Break | www.springbreak.com | Links to information on spring break |
| Internet Legal Resource Guide | www.ilrg.com/pre-law.html | Searches, Articles, Advice and more for Pre-laws |
| IRS Tax Information for Students | www.irs.gov/individuals/students/index.html | Information about education tax benefits from the IRS |
| IvyEssays | www.ivyessays.com | Free advice and fee-based essay services |
| Jesuit Colleges | www.ajcunet.edu | Browsable information on Jesuit colleges |
| Johns Hopkins School of Public Health | ocw.jhsph.edu | Online class notes for Johns Hopkins |
| Jones International University | www.jonesinternational.edu | Accredited Online university |

| Name | Address (URLs, etc.) | What's Inside |
|---|---|---|
| Kaplan's Test Prep | www.kaptest.com | Online test prep |
| Key Education Resources | www.key.com/education | Source for federal student loans |
| Kiplinger's Personal Finance Magazine | www.kiplinger.com | Investing for college |
| Laissaez-Faire Rankings | collegeadmissions.tripod.com | Colleges ranked by selectivity criteria |
| Law Jobs and Career Center | www.law.com/jsp/law/careercenter/index.jsp | Searches, Articles, Advice and more for Pre-laws |
| Live | www.live.com | Search engine and directory |
| LoanLocator | www.nslc.org | Track your student loans |
| LoanStar Student Program | www.loanstar.com | Source for federal student loans |
| Los Angeles Times' Education Coverage | www.latimes.com/education | Information about colleges in Southern California |
| Lycos | www.lycos.com | Search engine and catalog of the Web |
| Lycos Mail | mail.lycos.com | Commercial e-mail provider |
| MACH25 | www.collegenet.com/mach25 | Personalized scholarship-search service |
| Maclean's University Rankings | www.macleans.ca/universities | Canadian college rankings |
| Mail.com | www.mail.com | Commercial e-mail provider |
| Mail2Web | www.mail2web.com | Check e-mail while away from your computer |
| Mamma.com | www.mamma.com | Metasearch engine |
| Mapping Your Future | www.mapping-your-future.org/paying | About paying for college |
| MapQuest | www.mapquest.com | Get directions to college campuses |
| MBA Pathfinder | www.mba.com | Searches, Articles, Advice and more for Pre-bness |
| Metacrawler | www.metacrawler.com | Metasearch engine |
| Microsoft's home page | www.microsoft.com | Online help |
| Military.com | education.military.com/education-home | Information on military programs and careers |
| MIT OpenCourseWare | ocw.mit.edu | Online class notes for MIT |
| Money Magazine | www.money.cnn.com/pf/101/lessons/11 | Investing for college |
| Morningstar | www.morningstar.com | Investment advice |
| Motley Fool | www.fool.com | Investment advice |
| Mozilla Thunderbird | www.mozilla.org/projects/thunderbird | Access to newsgroups |
| mtvU | www.mtvu.com | Segments on college life |
| My (Military) Future | www.myfuture.com | Information on ROTC and other military programs |
| My College Guide | www.mycollegeguide.org | Searches, Articles, and more |
| My Rich Uncle | www.myrichuncle.com | Loan alternative |
| MyRoad.com | myroad.collegeboard.com/myroad/navigator.jsp | Searches, Career Information, and more |
| MySpace | www.myspace.com | Social networking site |

| Name | Address (URLs, etc.) | What's Inside |
|------|----------------------|---------------|
| NACAC Space Availability Survey | www.nacacnet.org/MemberPortal | Survey of NACAC colleges with openings |
| National Association for College Admission Counseling | www.nacacnet.org | News about higher education |
| National City | www.nationalcity.com | Source for federal student loans |
| National Commission for Cooperative Education | www.northeastern.edu/co-op | Online guide to co-op |
| National Directory of College Athletics | www.collegiatedirectories.com | E-mail addresses for college coaches |
| National Health Service Corps | nhsc.bhpr.hrsa.gov | Federal money for soon-to-be nurses and doctors |
| NCAA Guide for College-Bound Student-Athletes | www.ncaa.org | NCAA guide to scholarships, recruiting, and eligibility |
| NCAA Initial Eligibility Clearinghouse | www.ncaaclearinghouse.net | NCAA's academic eligibility clearinghouse |
| Nellie Mae | www.nelliemae.com | Source for private loans |
| Net M@nners | www.netmanners.com | An introduction to netiquette |
| NetDictionary | www.netdictionary.com | An Internet glossary |
| Netiquette | www.albion.com/netiquette | An introduction to netiquette |
| NetLingo | www.netlingo.com | An Internet glossary |
| Netscape's home page | www.netscape.com | Online help |
| New School Online University | online.newschool.edu | Online undergrad degree offered by New School |
| New York Times' Education Coverage | www.nytimes.com/pages/education.html | Information about colleges in NY and elsewhere |
| Newbies Anonymous: A Guide to the Internet | www.geocities.com/TheTropics/1945/index1.htm | An Internet introduction |
| News Link | www.newslink.org/statcamp.html | Links to newspapers around the country |
| Next Stop College | www.collegeboard.com/student/apply | Online applications |
| NextStudent | www.nextstudent.com | Source for private loans |
| NJCAA Guide for Athletes | www.njcaa.org | Sports programs at Junior Colleges |
| Notre Dame's OpenCourseWare | ocw.nd.edu | Online class notes for Notre Dame |
| Number2.com | www.number2.com | Free, online prep |
| Office of Postsecondary Education | www.ed.gov/about/offices/list/OPE/index.html | Technical resources from the Dept. of Education |
| Online Learning at Parkland College | online.parkland.edu | Links to online course providers, and courses |
| Online School Guide | www.directoryofschools.com | Catalog of online courses |
| Open Coursework Consortium | ocwconsortium.org | Index of schools offering online class notes |
| Pacific NW Scholarship Guide | www.collegeplan.org/cpnow/pnwguide/pnwguide.htm | Scholarship-search service for Pacific NW students |
| Personal Identification Number | www.pin.ed.gov | Apply for a personal identification number |
| Peterson's Best College Picks | www.bestcollegepicks.com | Database of college descriptions |
| Peterson's Distance Learning | www.petersons.com/distancelearning | Directory of online courses and programs |
| Peterson's Education Portal | www.petersons.com | Searches, Q-and-A areas, test prep and more |
| Pick-a-Prof | www.pick-a-prof.com | Faculty evaluations |

| Name | Address (URLs, etc.) | What's Inside |
|---|---|---|
| Plagiarism.org | www.plagiarism.org | Site to help professors catch online plagiarists |
| PNC Bank | www.eduloans.pncbank.com | Source for federal student loans |
| Prepstar | prepstar.com | Recruiting service |
| Presidential Freedom Scholars | www.learnandserve.gov/about/programs/pfs.asp | Information on Presidential Freedom Awards |
| Princeton Review | www.princetonreview.com | Searches, Articles, Test Prep and more |
| Princeton Review Test Prep | www.princetonreview.com/college/testPrep | Online test prep |
| Princeton Review's 366 Best Colleges | www.princetonreview.com/college/research/rankings/rankings.asp | Colleges ranked by students |
| Princeton Review's Advice | www.princetonreview.com/college/research/articleindex.asp | Advice for every step of the admission process |
| Princeton Review's Counselor-O-Matic | www.princetonreview.com/college | Database of college descriptions |
| Princeton Review's Eye on Apply | www.princetonreview.com/college/apply/eyeonapply/2007/default.asp | Online tour through the admission process |
| Princeton Review's Forums | discuss.princetonreview.com | Online discussions about choosing a college |
| Professional and Graduate Schools | www.gradschools.com/search.html | Links to home pages of graduate schools |
| PROFILE | profileonline.collegeboard.com | PROFILE Registration and Q-and-A |
| Quicken | www.quicken.com | Investment advice |
| Roomate Service.com | www.roommates.com | Roommate matching service |
| ROTC Headquarters | www.defenselink.mil/faq/pis/19.html | Information on ROTC |
| Sage Tuition Rewards Program | www.sagescholars.com | Investment program for parents |
| Sallie Mae | www.salliemae.com | Information on loans and the company itself |
| SAT Preparation Center | www.collegeboard.com/student/testing/sat | Standardized testing information and online test prep |
| Scholarship Research Network | www.smexpress.com | Scholarship-search service |
| Scholarship Scams | www.ftc.gov/bcp/conline/edcams/scholarship | Tips on spotting scams |
| ScholarStuff | www.scholarstuff.com | Searches, Q-and-A areas, and more |
| Scout USA | www.scoutusa.com | Recruiting service |
| Search | www.search.com | Metasearch engine |
| Secondary School Report Form | www.nacacnet.org/MemberPortal/products/forms.html | For guidance counselors |
| Security on Campus, Inc. | www.securityoncampus.org | Information about crime on campus |
| Servicemembers Opportunity College | www.soc.aascu.org | Online degrees for servicemembers and their families |
| SimpleTuition | www.simpletuition.com | Compare lenders |
| SmartMoney Magazine | www.smartmoney.com/college | Investing for college |
| Southern Regional Electronic Campus | www.electroniccampus.org | Online education at southern universities |
| Southwest Student Services | www.sssc.com | Source for federal student loans |
| State Higher-Education Agencies | wdcrobcolp01.ed.gov/Programs/EROD/org_list.cfm | Links to state-specific sites on financial aid |

| Name | Address (URLs, etc.) | What's Inside |
|---|---|---|
| Student Center | www.student.com | Articles, chat rooms, and links to college life sites |
| Student Counseling Virtual Pamphlet Collection | www.dr-bob.org/vpc | Links to virtual pamphlets on counseling topics |
| Student Doctor Network | www.studentdoctor.net | Searches, Articles, Advice and more for Pre-meds |
| Student Loan Funding | www.studentloanfunding.org | Source for federal student loans |
| StudentAdvantage.Com | www.studentadvantage.com | Discounts, articles, tools" |
| Studentjobs.gov | www.studentjobs.gov | Cooperative Education with the Federal Government |
| Students.Gov | www.students.gov | Department of Education's central student aid site |
| Study Hall | www.studyhall.com | Online test prep |
| Studyabroad.com | www.studyabroad.com | Browsable information on study-abroad programs |
| SunTrust Bank | www.suntrusteducation.com | Source for federal student loans |
| SUNY Learning Network | sln.suny.edu | Online education at State University of NY schools |
| Tax Benefits for Education | www.irs.gov/pub/irs-pdf/p970.pdf | Information about education tax benefits for students |
| Texas Guaranteed Student Loan Corporation | www.AdventuresinEducation.org | About paying for college |
| Texas Guaranteed Student Loan Corporation | www.tgslc.org | About paying for college |
| The Education Resources Institute | www.teri.org | Source for private loans |
| The Elements of Style | www.bartleby.com | The classic guide to effective writing |
| The List | www.thelist.com | List of Internet Service Providers |
| The Slot | www.theslot.com | Online style manual |
| The Street | www.thestreet.com | Investment advice |
| The U | www.theu.com | Virtual tours |
| Thesaurus | www.thesaurus.com | Online version of Roget's Thesaurus |
| Topix Education News | www.topix.net/education | News about higher education |
| Tufts' OpenCourseWare | ocw.tufts.edu | Online class notes for Tufts University |
| Tuition Management Systems | www.afford.com | Administers monthly-payment plans |
| TuitionPay | www.tuitionpay.com | Administers monthly-payment plans |
| Turn It In | www.turnitin.com | Site to help professors catch online plagiarists |
| U Magazine from Colleges.com | www.colleges.com/umagazine/index.html | Articles, chat and tools |
| U.S. News & World Report | www.usnews.com/sections/education | College rankings |
| U.S. News, Find Your Ideal School | www.usnews.com/usnews/edu/college/tools/search.php | Database of college descriptions |
| U.S. News College Forums | www.usnews.com/sections/education | The most vexing questions |
| U.S. Universities and Community Colleges | www.utexas.edu/world/univ | Links to home pages of colleges in the U.S. |
| United Negro College Fund | www.uncf.org | Scholarships typically for minority students |
| Universal Black Pages | www.ubp.com | Articles and links to sites about HBCUs |

| Name | Address (URLs, etc.) | What's Inside |
|---|---|---|
| Universal College Application | www.universalcollegeapp.com | Direct link to the electronic Universal College App |
| University of Phoenix | www.phoenix.edu | Online business education |
| UPromise | www.upromise.com | Investment program for parents |
| US Bank | www.usbank.com/studentloans | Source for federal student loans |
| Utah State's OpenCourseWare | ocw.usu.edu | Online class notes for Utah State |
| U-Wire | www.uwire.com | Links to top stories from student newspapers |
| | | |
| Vanguard | www.vanguard.com | Investment advice |
| Varsity Books | www.varsitybooks.com | Online source for college textbooks |
| Virtual University Gazette | www.geteducated.com/vug/index.asp | Electronic newsletter on distance education |
| | | |
| Wachovia | www.wachovia.com/personal | Source for federal student loans |
| Washington Post's Education Coverage | washingtonpost.com/wp-dyn/education/content/education | Information about colleges in Washington, DC |
| Wells Fargo | wellsfargo.com/per/accounts/student | Source for federal student loans |
| Western Governors University | www.wgu.edu | Virtual university |
| Wi-Fi Hotspots | www.openwifispots.com | List of Wi-Fi Hotspots |
| Women's College Coalition | www.womenscolleges.org | Links to home pages of women's colleges |
| Women's Sports Foundation | www.womenssportsfoundation.org | Sports information for women |
| Wordsmyth Educational Dictionary-Thesaurus | www.wordsmyth.net | Online dictionary |
| Wordsmyth S.A.T. Dictionary | www.lightlink.com/bobp/wedt/sat.htm | Dictionary of words that appear on SAT |
| World Wide Learn | www.worldwidelearn.com | Directory of online courses and programs |
| | | |
| Xanga | www.xanga.com | Social networking site |
| XAP Applications | www.xap.com/apply | Online applications |
| XAP's Mentor Web Sites | www.xap.com/gotocollege | Database of college descriptions |
| | | |
| Yahoo! | www.yahoo.com | Search engine and catalog of the Web |
| Yahoo! Mail | mail.yahoo.com | Commercial e-mail provider |
| Yahoo!'s College Listings-United States | dir.yahoo.com/Education/Higher_Education | Links to home pages of colleges in the U.S. |
| Yahoo!'s List of e-zines | dir.yahoo.com/News_and_Media/College_and_University | Links to more college-life magazines |
| Yahoo!'s List of Lenders | dir.yahoo.com/Education/Financial_Aid/Loans | Links to sites maintained by lenders |
| Yahoo!'s Overview of Distance Education | degrees.education.yahoo.com | Overview of distance education opportunities |
| | | |
| Zinch | www.zinch.com | Create an online profile for your colleges to view |
| ZixMail | www.zixcorp.com | Privacy enhancements to existing email |

# College Planning Guides from Octameron

**Don't Miss Out: The Ambitious Student's Guide to Financial Aid** ............................ **$13.00**
    Hailed as the top consumer guide to student aid, *Don't Miss Out* covers scholarships, loans, and personal finance strategies. It will save readers hundreds, if not thousands of dollars in college costs.

**The A's and B's of Academic Scholarships** ................................................. **$13.00**
    Money for being bright! This book describes 100,000 awards offered by nearly 1200 colleges. Best of all, most of these (which must be used at the sponsoring school) are not based on financial need.

**Loans and Grants from Uncle Sam** ............................................................. **$8.00**
    Increase your eligibility for federal student aid. This guide describes it all—the aid application process as well as loans and grants for students, parents and health professionals.

**Financial Aid FinAncer: Expert Answers to College Financing Questions** ................. **$8.00**
    Learn how special family circumstances impact on student aid.

**The Winning Edge: The Student-Athlete's Guide to College Sports** ........................... **$9.00**
    It's all here. Scholarship opportunities. NCAA rules and regulations. Advice from coaches. Sample athletic resumes. Strategies, timetables, and worksheets—all to help you take your sport to college!

**Financial Aid Officers: What They Do—To You and For You** ........................................ **$5.00**
    Should you accept your award package as offered? Can you request it be changed, or increased? Knowledgeable dealings with FAOs can result in more money. This book shows you how.

**Behind the Scenes: An Inside Look at the College Admission Process** ..................... **$8.00**
    Ed Wall, former Dean of Admission at Amherst College, offers sage advice and detailed profiles of successful applicants. An invaluable view from inside on how the selection process really works.

**Do It Write: How to Prepare a Great College Application** .............................................. **$7.00**
    Personalize your essays so they stand out from the crowd. Author Gary Ripple is the former Admission Director at Lafayette College and the College of William and Mary

**College Match: A Blueprint for Choosing the Best School for You** .......................... **$11.00**
    Author Steve Antonoff combines dozens of easy-to-use worksheets with lots of practical advice to make sure you find schools that meet your needs and your preferences.

**Campus Pursuit: Making the Most of the Visit and Interview** ..................................... **$6.00**
    Nervous about your interview? In his companion book to *Do-It Write*, Gary Ripple gives advice that will help you shine, as well as show you how to maximize the benefits of a campus visit.

**College.edu: On-Line Resources for the Cyber-Savvy Student** ................................... **$11.00**
    Lost in Cyberspace? *College.edu* takes you to hundreds of useful sites on admission and financial aid, giving you Internet tips and warnings along the way.

**Campus Daze: Easing the Transition from High School to College** ........................... **$8.00**
    Learn what to expect during your first year of college and how to succeed starting on Day One. Author George Gibbs is the former Dean of Admission and Freshmen at Muhlenberg College.

**College Majors That Work** ............................................................................................ **$10.00**
    Get in. Get out. Get a job. Worksheets help match a student's goals and expectations with the right college major and explores how that choice plays out in the real world—influencing both career and lifestyle options. Written by Michael P. Viollt, President of Robert Morris College (IL),

**Calculating Expected Family Contribution (EFC) Software** .......................................... **$45.00**
    Estimate how much you will be expected to pay for college. This Windows-compatible CD-Rom software holds data on hundreds of families and let's you analyze different income and asset scenarios.

---

# Ordering Information

    **Send orders to**: Octameron Associates, PO Box 2748, Alexandria, VA 22301, or contact us at: 703-836-5480 (voice), 703-836-5650 (fax), octameron@aol.com.

    You may also order online at www.octameron.com.

    **Postage and Handling:** Please include $3.00 for the first publication, $1.00 for each additional, to a maximum of $6.00 per order.

    **Method of Payment:** Payment must accompany order. We accept checks, money orders, American Express, Visa and MasterCard.

    If ordering by credit card, please include the card number and its expiration date.